Longhair Cats

BARRON'S

Woodbury, N.Y. • London • Toronto • Sydney

Longhair Cats

by Grace Pond

Technical Consultant:
Dr. Matthew M. Vriends

Photographer:
Paddy Cutts/Animals Unlimited

90010

Cover illustrations: front, Ryshworth Rumtumtugger (Red
Self Longhair): back, Chirunga Silver Mist (Pewter Longhair
kitten).

The publisher expresses appreciation
to The Cat Fanciers' Association, Inc.,
1309 Allaire Avenue, Ocean, NJ 07712,
for permission to use portions of the
association's *Show Standards* (May 1983-
April 1984).

First U.S. Edition 1984 by Barron's Educational Series,
Inc.
Text © Grace Pond 1983
British edition published by B. T. Batsford, Ltd.
4 Fitzhardinge Street
London W1H OAH

All inquiries should be addressed to:
Barron's Educational Series, Inc.
113 Crossways Park Drive
Woodbury, New York 11797

Library of Congress Catalog Card No. 84-9198
International Standard Book No. 0-8120-2923-2

Library of Congress Cataloging in Publication Data

Pond, Grace.
    Longhair cats.

    Previous ed.: The longhaired cat.
    Includes index.
    1. Longhair cats.   I. Vriends, Matthew M., 1937-
II. Pond, Grace.   Longhaired cat.   III. Title.
SF449.L65P66   1984   636.8'3   84-9198
ISBN 0-8120-2923-2

PRINTED IN ITALY

4 5 6   0 4 1   9 8 7 6 5 4 3 2 1

636.8
P796 c

1/86

Contents

1 The History of the Longhair Cats

As far as can be ascertained, the first domesticated cats, for which Egypt is generally given the credit, had short fur, although there is still much mystery about their beginnings. There is just as much mystery about the origin of the cats with long coats. The Comte Georges de Buffon (1707-88), a French naturalist, wrote a book which was translated, abridged and published in England in 1792 as *Natural History*. In his book he included some pages on cats with long fur. He spoke of long-coated cats in Spain and also those in Chorafan and Syria, and went on to say that "when wild cats are tamed their coats become longer, finer and most copious, with color changes." He believed that, by taking cats with the most white in their coats and with the longest fur, it was possible to produce the Angora to order. This is now known to be the first step in the selective breeding of longhairs. He wrote too of cats in China with long fur and pendant ears, which were great favorites with the Chinese ladies. His reference to the Angoras is one of the earliest; exactly when these cats and others with long fur, such as the Persians, first evolved is still a matter of surmise.

In all probability a kitten with a fluffy coat was born in a shorthair litter; that is, it was a mutation, and because of its unusual appearance it was kept. Natural matings with a litter brother or sister or with the father could result in further such kittens. The strange thing is that this seems to have happened at about the same time in various parts of the world such as confined mountainous areas in Turkey, Persia (now Iran), China, India, Afghanistan and the Soviet Union. It is possible that there may have been such cats for centuries, but because of the inaccessibility of these areas, the few travellers reaching them, and the lesser interest in cats in comparison with the unusual larger wild animals, no mention was made of them until the sixteenth century. There are many stories and legends about the Siamese and similar cats being found in temples or in the royal courts, but of the longhairs only the Birmans were associated with a similar history.

Early travellers, pilgrims and seafarers must have been instrumental in bringing the first long-coated cats into Europe from the East. Pietro de la Velle is said to have introduced cats with long fur into Italy in the middle of the sixteenth century, and at the end of that century Nicholas Claude Fabri de Peirese, the naturalist, was responsible for bringing the Angora cats into France, where de Buffon must have seen them. Later these cats came into Britain, and were known as French cats, which seemed logical at the time!

Gr Ch Deebank Blackjack, a Black Persian with an outstanding broad head. Owner Miss Jacqui Stevens; breeder Miss M.F. Bull.

7

Grand Champion
Blue-eyed White
Persian—Chirunga
Polarice, with his
little pewter kitten.
Owner and breeder
Mrs. Kayes.

In 1868 Charles Ross, an early writer on cats, gave details of the various long-hair breeds in Britain; this was before the first official show in 1871. He wrote that "Angoras have silvery hair of a fine silken texture, but some are yellowish and others olive, approaching the color of the lion." The Persian cat, he wrote, had "hair long and very silky, perhaps more so than the Cat of Angora, differently coloured being of a fine uniform grey on the upper part with the texture of the fur as soft as silk and the lustre glossy." He said that the Chinese cat had beautifully glossed fur, variegated with black and yellow, and usually with pendulous ears, and referred to the Spanish cat or Tortoiseshell with fur of moderate length, with colors of pure black, white and reddish orange. Dr. Gordon Stables, an author and early cat fancier, referred to the longhairs in his own book *The Domestic Cat* published in 1876, but called them the Asiatic cats. He wrote that they could be found in the same colors and variations in color and markings as those of the shorthair European cats, that is in blue, white, black and tabbies, all with "long pelages and good brushes" (coats and tails).

The most famous cat expert of that time, and the man to whom the Cat Fancy all over the world owes its very being, was Harrison Weir, an artist, an author, and a Fellow of the Royal Horticultural Society. Not only was he responsible for the first official cat show ever held, but he drew up the Points of Excellence, now known as the standards, by which cats could be judged; he was also one of the first cat judges. In his book published in 1889, he gave details of the Angora, the Persian and the Russian; the latter, he said, had "the woolliest coat of them all" and were "mostly dark tabby." In his Points he dis-

tinguished between the fur, "being fine, silky and very soft in the Persian, slightly woolly texture in the Angora and still more so in the Russian." Referring to the tails he said that those of the Persians had hair long and silky throughout, but somewhat longer at the base; the Angora was like the brush of a fox, but longer in the hair; and the Russian equally long in hair but more full at the end, "tail shorter rather blunt, like a tassel." From a mixture of these early longhairs, expert and planned breeding has produced in 100 years many color variations and coat patterns in the cats with long coats. The Cat Fanciers' Association, Inc., for instance, accepts 39 Persian colors, 12 Himalayan colors, and 4 Birman colors.

Of course it was not surprising that the interest of the public in the first cat show, held in London's Crystal Palace in 1871, was tremendous. Due to its great success the show became an annual event. Some years later cat shows were being held all over England, and cat clubs were formed. In 1895 the first cat show in the United States was held in New York City; four years later the beginning of an organized fancy occurred in Chicago.

In the early days of the Cat Fancy little was known about breeding for particular colors and as the cats from Persia had longer fur and broader heads with smaller ears, and the kittens in particular had 'chocolate box' appeal, they began to be preferred to the Angoras, with their smaller heads, larger ears and longer noses. There must have been cross-matings, as eventually the Angora vanished and all the cats with long fur were known as Persians. In fact one cat judge, the breeder and author Miss Frances Simpson, in her book *The Book of the Cat* (1902) wrote that "the differences between Angoras and Per-

sians are of so fine a nature that I must be pardoned if I ignore the class of cat commonly called Angora, which seems gradually to have disappeared from our midst."

In the early 1900s Whites were the most popular variety in Britain as well as in the United States and many were exhibited at Crystal Palace (London) or at the Beresford Cat Club Show. At the latter there were so many entries that the organizers had to divide the classification into Blue-eyed and Golden-eyed Persians, and then again into male and female. At that time Mrs. C. Locke gained recognition by showing a number of exquisite Whites. She notified the show authorities that the first White she had owned was brought to her from Persia by a traveller. The eyes of this gorgeous cat were amber, which, according to Mrs. Locke, "showed that White cats brought from their native land did not always have Blue eyes." And, indeed, it is a fact that descendants of this White, amber-eyed cat, mated both to blue-eyed and amber-eyed cats produced blue-eyed kittens. It remains true that White Persians are still extremely popular in the United States.

Blacks have always been and still are very popular in our country. Their quality increased appreciably after World War II. The beautiful cats of Mrs. Bess H. Moore, and especially her Grand Champion Pied Piper of Barbe Bleue, which became Cat of the Year in 1951, come to mind immediately. And let us especially not forget Mr. Richard Gebhardt's Grand Champion Vel-vene Voo Doo of Silva-Wyte, which was the great-grandsire of Pied Piper, and is believed to have been one of the most outstanding Blacks ever seen, and—above all—probably the greatest sire of all time. Voo Doo became Cat of the Year in 1959.

Cross-matings between Blacks and Silvers (Chinchillas and Silver Tabbies) are said to have produced the original Smokes, which were far more numerous at the turn of the century than they are today. Harrison Weir gave the original Tabbies as Brown, Silver, Light Gray, and White. The Reds were not mentioned in the early Tabbies, but in a very short time, the only colors recognized in the Tabbies were Brown, Silver, and Red, all without White.

The Chinchillas are thought to have originated from lightly marked Silver Tabbies and Blues, but they were certainly of a different coloring from the magnificent specimens seen at the shows today. Miss Simpson wrote of these early Chinchillas as having "the fur at the roots a peculiar light silver, not white.... and this shades to a slightly darker tone—a sort of bluish lavender—at the tips of the coats."

The Tortoiseshells, a female-only variety, had a standard similar to that of today, that is, the coats should be uniformly distributed in black, red, and cream, and as bright as possible. Those cats seen at the early shows were, according to a female judge, not outstanding, although she complained that they were invariably given "some mark of distinction" when they were judged by "the professional men judges," as Tortoiseshells were the men's favorite breed. We might add that men seem still to like Torties today.

Very few Bi-Color cats appear to have been shown. For years they were not recognized, but in later years, fanciers realized that Bi-Colors would be very useful in breeding for Calicos, another female-only variety. One well-known breeder concentrated on producing them, and they now appear in a number of colors, and have full Champion status. The early Cal-

Opposite Ryshworth Rumtumtugger, a male Red Self Persian with a coat of a very striking color. Owner and breeder Mrs. Pam Sadler.

icos were few and far between, as producing them was very much a matter of chance.

These were, among a few others, the varieties seen at the early shows, and they were considered most exotic in their day. As the years have gone by the type has improved, and shorter, flatter noses have become fashionable in Persians. Some of today's cats, in fact, have noses that are too short, but this can be rectified by careful breeding.

In almost 100 years since the beginning of the United States Cat Fancy, by accidental cross-matings and later by selective and planned breeding, it has been

possible to produce many longhair pedigree colors and breeds. The early varieties have in most cases been improved in type and coloring. Man-made varieties, such as the Himalayans, have been bred, and the Turkish and the Birmans have been introduced by importation. Chocolates, the Lilacs, and the Cameos are all appearing on the show bench. Much improved knowledge of genetics, particularly in the last decade or two, has enabled breeders to produce specific colors and breeds beyond the dreams of the early fanciers.

Typically patched Tortoiseshell Persian, Hopecott Nicola: this is one of the female-only varieties. Owner and breeder Mr. and Mrs. C. Green.

13

2 Shows, Show Activity, and the Cat Fancy

In 1871, in the reign of Queen Victoria (who later owned two Blue Persians), the first official cat show to be held anywhere in the world took place at the Crystal Palace in London. The show was the brainchild of Mr. Harrison Weir, who felt that such an event would bring to the public the realization of how beautiful cats could be. He could never have visualized what he was starting, that in little more than 100 years cat shows would be held in most countries throughout the world, that cats and kittens would be exported from one country to another sometimes for sums involving quite a few hundred dollars and that there would be innumerable organizations providing cat foods, cat accessories, and cat medication of various kinds.

When the doors opened on that July morning there were hundreds waiting to see the 170 cats and kittens that were being exhibited for the first time ever. These included Angoras, Persians, two Siamese, and even a Wild Cat from Scotland, which had lost part of a front paw, and yet was still so fierce that a dozen men failed to get the poor creature out of its basket. The show was reported in full by newspapers, with the *Illustrated London News* including a number of drawn illustrations of many of the cats. There were complaints that there were so many people

there that for some, it proved impossible to see the cats.

Mr. Harrison Weir, his brother Jenner, and the Rev. Cumming Macdona judged the exhibits, and 54 prizes, with the grand total value of £57 15s, were awarded. The cats shown included Crimean cats, Prussian cats and Algerian cats as well as Persians. It is presumed that they came from these various countries, hence the names.

Such was the popularity of the first show, and the public demand, that another show was quickly organized in December. In the next few years there followed a spate of cat shows in such towns as Edinburgh, Crawley, Brighton, Manchester, and Birmingham as well as London. Soon shows were being held in the United States and other parts of the world. Quarantine regulations did not exist and it was possible to send cats and kittens from one country to another to be shown. In these early days there were no pedigree cats as such, for no records were kept of ancestry, and it was soon realized that to put everything on a proper basis it would be necessary to have some kind of register with details of breeding and parentage, and the different varieties.

In 1887 the National Cat Club came into being, with Mr. Harrison Weir as the president and many august personages and

A cat may always be washing, but daily grooming is still necessary for the removal of loose hairs. This cat is being prepared for a British show.

15

members of society on the committee. The club started a register and was the world's first governing body, with cats and kittens being accepted at the shows only if they were registered, for which the charge was one shilling. The shows were held under the sponsorship of the National Cat Club and the charge for each class entered was 5 shillings, a lot of money in those days. Similar rulings applied then as today: cats would be disqualified if not registered, or if they had not been in the possession of the exhibitor for at least 14 days prior to the show, if the wrong pedigree was given or if the age of the cat or kitten was incorrectly given. Free use of powder on the coat would also mean disqualification as could "dyeing the chins of tabby cats and the white spots on self-colour-cats," which would also certainly be the case today.

The first large American cat show was held in Madison Square Gardens, New York, in 1895. Organized by an Englishman, Mr. J. Hyde, it followed similar lines to the Crystal Palace shows in Britain and was an immediate success. The Chicago Cat Club was founded in 1899 but was short-lived, being ousted by the Beresford Cat Club founded by Mrs. Clinton Locke. It was named after the English breeder, Lady Marcus Beresford, who was interested in many varieties and frequently exported outstanding cats to the United States.

At first cat breeding and exhibiting seemed to be purely the prerogative of the wealthy and of "high society," with fanciers such as the Lady Decies, who showed many longhair cats including Ch Fulmer Zaida, winner of over 150 prizes, and the Lady Marcus Beresford, who was said to have about 150 cats, and travelled around the country to the various shows with a retinue of servants to look after them. The Hon. Mrs. McLaren Morrison was well known for her Black cat Satan and often exhibited 14 Blacks at one show. The patron of the National Cat Club was HRH Princess Victoria of Schleswig Holstein. As Queen Victoria herself visited shows with the Prince of Wales, later Edward VII, pedigree cats became "status symbols," especially as the Princess of Wales, afterwards Queen Alexandra, was also a cat-lover. Later classes were put on for the "working classes" at reduced fees and for pet cats only (it was felt that they would not be able to afford pedigree cats).

In those days there were no vaccinations or injections available to protect the cats and kittens from the killer diseases which were then prevalent. Frequently, after a show, fanciers would lose all their stock, never thinking to isolate the exhibit they were bringing home from the show. Often too, they would go and buy another kitten immediately only to have this one die from the infection in a very short time. Death could come so swiftly that the owners were quite sure that their cats had been poisoned at the show. In the early days the judges never wore overalls to protect their clothing, as all British judges do today. Skirts were long, sweeping the ground, and hygiene was of a very low standard. World War I saw fewer shows and very little breeding, but by 1920 the Cat Fancy was beginning to pick up again, and more shows were held. The National Cat Club continued to hold its shows at the Crystal Palace until 1936 when the building burned down the day before the show was due to be held. However, the show did go on in another hall after the show manager sent telegrams to everyone concerned, and it was its usual success.

Over the years more varieties were recognized and the Fancy flourished, many more fanciers taking up breeding and more clubs being formed. Unfortunately World War II nearly rang its death knell, hundred of cats being put down by the often-reluctant vets and famous studs being neutered. Ever resilient, a few breeders managed to struggle on and they formed the nucleus of the now enormous Cat Fancy in Britain today. Shortly after the war ended the Notts and Derby Cat Club put on a cat show, but unfortunately many of the exhibits subsequently died from infection. The tragedy alerted fanciers again to the dangers of showing and shows were reestablished very slowly. Fortunately, in a year or two vaccines were being produced which did and still do keep some killer diseases to a minimum, and modern hygiene has also helped. Today it is not possible to exhibit without a current certificate for protection against feline infectious enteritis for each cat and kitten shown. However, it is still wise to isolate an exhibit brought home from a show for some days rather than allowing it to immediately mix with other cats, as there are still other illnesses, even a common cold, which can follow a show and can be given to other cats unless specific precautions are taken.

The majority of the American and Canadian cat shows are conducted along the same general rules and stipulations as those in Britain. When planning to take part in a show, be wise and pick one that is within easy driving distance of your home. The first step, however, is writing to the secretary of the club who organizes the show, requesting an entry form. The entry blank then must be filled out properly; in the case of a show affiliated with the CFA, not only the name of the organizing show must be given on the form, but also the class in which the cat must be entered: Non-Championship, Championship, or Premiership. Those three classes are in turn divided into subclasses. The show rules of the CFA define the following.

Non-Championship Classes

a) The *Kitten Class* is for any kitten, male or female, not less than 4 months but under 8 calendar months old on the opening day of the show, which, if an adult, would be eligible to compete in a Championship Class. Kittens are not eligible for any "Bests" in show except Kitten awards.

b) The *AOV* (Any Other Variety) *Class* is for any registered, adult, whole cat or registered kitten, the ancestry of which entitles it to Championship competition, but which does not (colorwise, coatwise, or, in the case of Manx, tailwise) conform to the accepted show standard. An AOV entry is eligible only for awards in the AOV class of its own breed.

c) The *Provisional Breed Class* is for any registered cat or registered kitten of a breed not accepted for Championship competition when CFA has approved a provisional standard for that breed. Cats entered in the Provisional Breed Class are eligible only for awards in the Provisional Breed Class. Provisional Breeds shall compete separately as Kittens, Altered Cats, or Adult, whole cats.

d) The *Miscellaneous* (Non-Competitive) *Class* is for any registered cat or registered kitten of a breed not yet accepted for Provisional Breed competition.

e) The *Household Pet Class* is for any domestic kitten or altered cat entry not otherwise eligible. Household Pets are eligible only for awards in the Household Pet Class. Household Pets are to be judged separately from all other cats, solely on beauty and condition. Feral cats or feral cat-domestic cat hybrid crosses are not eligible for entry.

Black Smoke—Ch
Shirar Montgomery,
showing glimpses of
the contrasting
undercoat. Owner
and breeder Mr. and
Mrs. G. Martin.

Championship Classes

a) The *Open Class* is for CFA registered cats of either sex, 8 months or over, except cats that have completed requirements for Championship confirmation. When a cat has completed requirements for confirmation, it is ineligible for the Open Class at any subsequent show.

b) The *Champion Class* is for cats that have completed Championships in this Association, and for which the required Championship claim has been mailed to the Central Office.

c) The *Grand Champion Class* is for cats that have completed Grand Championships in CFA.

Premiership Classes

a) Premiership Classes are for CFA registered neutered or spayed cats, 8 months old or over, that would, as whole cats, be eligible to compete in the Championship classes.

b) The following classes will be recognized for neuters and spays of each Championship Color Class: Grand Premier, Premier, and Open. The eligibility for each class will be determined in the same manner as for the corresponding class in Championship competition.

Wins made in Championship competition may not be transferred to Premiership records. However, titles won in Championship competition are retained.

When is a cat eligible for entry? According to the CFA, "Any cat or kitten of sound health not less than 4 calendar months old on the opening day of a show . . . sanctioned by CFA . . . Any cat or kitten from a house or cattery where there has been fungus or any infectious or contagious illness within 21 days prior to the opening date of a show is ineligible for entry, and, should entry have been made prior to the onset of any such condition,

such entry is ineligible for admission into the showroom." It is understandable that "only cats registered with CFA are eligible for entry in the Championship and Premiership Competitive Categories and the Provisional Breed, Miscellaneous (Non-Competitive), or AOV Classes. The Show Management is expressly prohibited from accepting a Championship, Premiership, Provisional Breed Miscellaneous (Non-Competitive), or AOV entry unless the official Entry Blank contains a registration number. It is the responsibility of the owner to enter the cat with its proper registration number as shown on the registration certificate." Additionally:

Each cat must be entered in the breed under which it is registered.

When an officiating Judge is the breeder of a cat or kitten, such cat or kitten is not eligible for competition in that Judge's ring. This rule shall not apply to shows in Hawaii and Japan.

A neutered or spayed kitten is not eligible for entry.

A cat that has completed requirements for Championship or Premiership confirmation is ineligible for further competition until claim has been filed for Championship or Premiership.

A cat that has won a Championship or Premiership in one color class is not eligible for entry in a different color class except that a cat that has been confirmed as a Champion or Premier in one color class and, after confirmation, changes color, may be shown in the correct color class by notifying the Central Office of the color change and payment of a fee. . . . The cat may then compete as an open in the proper color class. The Central Office must confirm the color class change prior to competition in a new color class. Only one change will be permitted.

A cat not having all its physical properties—eyes, ears, legs, tail (except Manx), claws, for

The bustle of a modern cat show, the English National Cat Club Show in 1982.

example, is not eligible for entry subject to the following exceptions:

a) cats in Premiership classes that have been altered; and
b) altered cats that are eligible for adult Household Pet classes.

An adult male must have at least one descended testicle to be eligible for entry.

Male kittens are not required to have descended testicles.

The Show Committee may refuse to accept an entry received after midnight of the advertised date for the closing of entries, or after the advertised limit of entries has been reached.

The Show Committee may permit kittens 4 months old or older, or cats, to be entered for exhibition or sale.

No more than two kittens or one cat may be benched in a single cage whether entered for exhibition, for sale, or for competition.

No cat or kitten shall be benched at more than one show per week (Monday through Sunday inclusive).

From the above it becomes apparent that it is important to fill in the entry blank properly before returning it to the secretary of the organizing club. And don't forget to pay the entry fee! According to the CFA, "an entry must be the property of the person who is shown on the Entry Blank as the owner. The records in the Central Office are conclusive where the ownership of the entry is concerned. If title is transferred between the date of entry and the date of the show, the transfer must be reported to the Show Secretary. It is essential that transfer of ownership papers be filed with the Central Office immediately upon transfer of title. The claws of each entry must be clipped prior to benching."

Depending upon the rules of the organizing cat association or federation—and most show rules are fairly simple and straightforward—the cat that one intends to enter may or may not have to be vetted-in on arrival at the show. It is advisable to know what exactly is expected! The CFA is quite clear about the health requirements. It advises strongly to have any cat or kitten entering a show inoculated before entry by a licensed veterinarian against feline enteritis, feline rhinotracheitis, and calici viruses. CFA has an extensive rule, titled "Article V: Procedures Prior to Benching," which is of the utmost importance to the fancier:

Procedures for shows with veterinarian inspection.

a) For a show with veterinarian inspection, a licensed practising Veterinarian acting for the club must examine each cat or kitten, including household pets and entries for sale or exhibition, prior to benching and shall disqualify any cat that shows evidence of fungus, fleas, ear mites, or any infectious or contagious illness.

b) In the event that the Veterinarian is unable to officiate or does not appear at the designated time for benching inspection and a substitute Veterinarian cannot be engaged to perform the benching inspection, the show shall be declared a show without veterinarian inspection. Those exhibitors who so request shall be reimbursed for all entry fees for the entries present, and their entries shall be marked "absent."

c) Cats arriving at a show the night before the show opens must be examined by the Veterinarian that night or placed in a room separated from the showroom until the Veterinarian is in attendance.

d) The owner or the owner's agent of each cat considered by the Veterinarian to be in good health shall be issued a card to that effect and thereby benched.

Inspection subsequent to benching for shows with veterinarian inspection.

a) The Veterinarian has the power to order the immediate removal of any sick cat from the show. Such cat will be entitled to all prizes awarded to it prior to the decision of the Veterinarian.

b) Any exhibitor, Judge, or Show Committee member suspecting any cat of having contagious or infectious illness may report same to the Show Manager, and it will be the duty of the Show Manager to remove such cat to a room apart from the regular showroom until the Veterinarian can pass upon the health of the suspected animal. In the event that the Veterinarian confirms and/or diagnoses contagious or infectious illness, the entry shall be disqualified, but awards received prior to the decision shall stand. If the Veterinarian certifies the entry as free from contagious or infectious illness, it shall be returned to the showroom and to normal competition. It shall be the responsibility of the owner or agent of the suspected Entry to obtain a Veterinarian's services although Show Management shall provide as much assistance as possible.

In this respect it is interesting to note that the CFA, founded in 1906, is by far the largest registering body in the United States, with more than 575 member clubs and responsible for more than half the vast number of shows in this country. It held its two first impressive shows in 1906: one in Buffalo and one in Detroit. (Although the CFA has no individual memberships, all members of local affiliated cat clubs become automatically associated.) The great distances involved in our country soon made it impracticable to have only one body registering and sponsor-

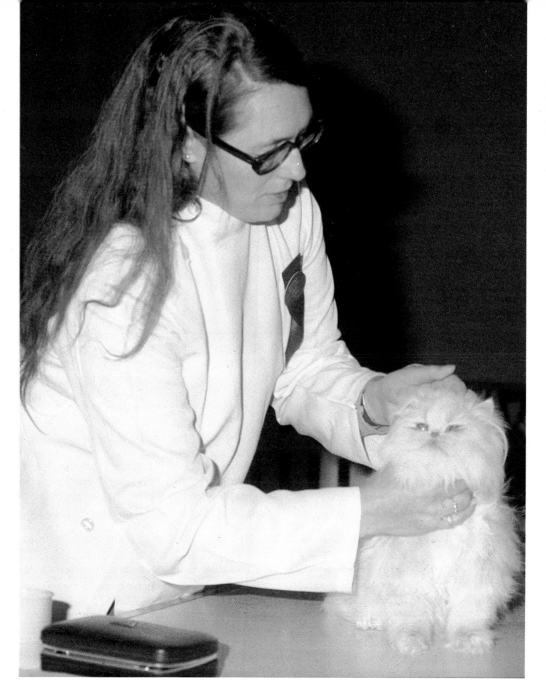

Vetting-in is the preliminary inspection of competitors, essential for the welfare of all cats at the show to avoid the spread of infection.

ing shows, and others evolved. In 1919, the Cat Fanciers' Federation (CFF) was formed; the United Cat Fanciers (UCF) was founded in 1946, the American Cat Fanciers' Association (ACFA) in 1955, the National Cat Fanciers' Association (NCFA) in 1960, the Crown Cat Fanciers' Federation (CCFF) in 1965, and the Independent Cat Federation (ICF) in 1969. The Canadian Cat Association (1961) is exclusively Canadian, but several of the other associations hold shows in both the United States and Canada, while the CFA is also associated with certain shows in Japan. There are also a number of clubs not connected with any association.

Several of the federations have banded together, and are known collectively as the International Cat Associations. They accept cats registered with any association at their shows, which is a considerable advantage to the exhibitors; otherwise, their cats would have to be registered with the specific organization running the show they wish to enter.

Fortunately — as said before — the standards accepted are very much the same throughout the United States, as is the system of running the shows, which differs considerably from that in Britain.

The most prestigious shows in our country are usually held between the months of September and February. One of the first things with which a cat must become familiar is its show-type cage. Even more important, of course, is to bring the animal into top condition: check its ears, clip its claws, clean its body so it is free from dirt and fleas. It is understandable that a female cat that is obviously pregnant doesn't belong at a show.

A couple of hours before the show the cat should not receive any food, but as soon as it is placed in its show-cage, and the animal has settled down, some of its favorite light food can be presented.

When you arrive in the show-hall one of the officials will hand you a card on which your name, your cat's name, and the number of its cage is typed. You will also get a schedule of the various classes, and the names of the judges (usually four) and their location in the show-hall.

As soon as your cat is examined and okayed by a veterinarian (when a vet is assigned to the show), and safely placed in its show-cage, it is wise to purchase a catalog, so you will know who your competitors are.

Knowing that your cat is comfortable, it is time to locate the place where your cat will be judged. This place (the ring) is a large table with a small platform; behind it is the judge. On either side, behind the judge and in a U-shaped setup, are about ten cages in which the cats will be placed by a steward, prior to judging. At one side of that same table sits a clerk whose duties include keeping records, entering your name, and checking all the information against notes in the catalog.

The judge has a looseleaf notebook in which all entries are properly recorded. Then each class is called on the loudspeaker and the cats are placed in the cages behind the judge. These cages have the numbers of the corresponding cats attached to the front.

When all cats are ready to be judged, the judge will begin his examination. Each cat will be taken out of the cage by the judge or the steward, and situated on the little platform in the center of the table. A thorough examination follows. After each examination the judge's hands and the table are disinfected. The final decision is reached by comparison and point evaluation against the breed standard. The ribbons are awarded and the cats are then retrieved by their proud (or disappointed) owners or agents. In turn, the cages behind the judge's table are disinfected, and a new group of anxious cat owners will be called. It goes without saying that the decision of the judge is always and inevitably final.

The judges are paid according to the number of exhibits judged and receive travelling and hotel expenses. In Britain the judges give their services free, receiving only travelling expenses and hotel expenses for one night should this be required. Would-be judges have to undergo an intensive training program before being considered for the position.

In Canada the first recorded show was held in Toronto in 1906, sponsored by the Royal Canadian Cat Club but it was not until 1961 that the Canadian Cat Association started registering cats for the first time in Canada.

There had been a great deal of interest in cats before this date and many cat clubs were already in existence but the cats were registered with one of the American organizations. World War II saw, as in Britain, almost the complete cessation of pedigree cat breeding and cat shows, but things started up again shortly after the war ended, with a number of breeders soon producing excellent kittens once again. Shows were held once more, with the Canadian National Cat Club sponsoring the important shows held at the Canadian National Exhibitions, an annual exhibition including shows for all kinds of animals. In 1968 the Canadian National Cat Club was disbanded and the Royal Canadian Cat Club took over the responsibility for the cat show at the exhibition.

Shows in Canada are run along lines similar to those in the United States and both countries participate freely in each other's cat activities. Cats from Canada may be shown in the United States, and vice versa, judges from both countries often officiating at the same show.

Interest in pedigree cats increases each year in Canada, with more and more clubs coming into being and more shows being held.

Generally the shows in the United States and Canada are not as large as those held in the British Isles but the distances to be travelled are very great and many exhibitors go by plane for quickness, although others travel many hundreds of miles by car. The shows are usually two-day affairs.

For exhibitors showing cats both in Canada and in the United States there is the added excitement of winning one of the much-coveted awards, that of International Champion and International Grand Champion. A cat must be a Champion or a Grand Champion in each country to achieve this feat.

3 The Longhair Varieties Today

It is said that the Persian cat is the oldest longhair variety in Europe. However, there are documents which provide evidence that the Angora cat, with its origin in Turkey, was already known in Europe around 1520. The Persian cats, or Longhairs as they are now officially called in Britain, are descendants from the Angora. Ever since the first cat show was held in England in 1871, most ailurophiles regard the Persian as a modern breed. And indeed since that year a somewhat scientific and selective breeding program started. At first the cats' noses were longish, the heads narrow, the ears large, and the bodies rangy, but careful breeding over the years has brought about changes in type and characteristics. These aristocratic cats now have broad heads with small neat ears, short broad noses, big round eyes, ruffs framing the heads, cobby bodies on sturdy legs, long flowing coats, and short full tails without kinks. Some may have noses a little long and eyes somewhat small. These faults only matter if the cat is to be shown or used for breeding; most pet owners consider their own perfect.

By 1903 most of the "real" Angoras disappeared and, as it were, merged into Persians. Today Europe and England consider each Persian color a separate breed, while the United States looks at them as Persians of different colors.

Following is the official *Show Standard* of the Cat Fanciers' Association, Inc., and some helpful comments.

Persian

Point Score

Head (Including size and shape of 30
  eyes, ear shape and set)
Type (Including shape, size, bone and. . . . 20
  length of tail)
Coat 10
Balance 5
Refinement 5
Color. 20
Eye Color 10

In all tabby varieties, the 20 points for color are to be divided 10 for markings and 10 for color.

HEAD: Round and massive, with great breadth of skull. Round face with round underlying bone structure. Well set on a short, thick neck.

EARS: Small, round-tipped, tilted forward, and not unduly open at the base. Set far apart, and low on the head, fitting into (without distorting) the rounded contour of the head.

EYES: Large, round, and full. Set far apart and brilliant, giving a sweet expression to the face.

NOSE: Short, snub, and broad. With "break."

CHEEKS: Full.

JAWS: Broad and powerful.

CHIN: Full and well-developed.

BODY: Of cobby type, low on the legs, deep in the chest, equally massive across shoulders and rump, with a short well-rounded middle piece. Large or medium in size. Quality the determining consideration rather than size.

BACK: Level.

LEGS: Short, thick, and strong. Forelegs straight.

PAWS: Large, round, and firm. Toes carried close, five in front and four behind.

TAIL: Short, but in proportion to body length. Carried without a curve and at an angle lower than the back.

COAT: Long and thick, standing off from the body. Of fine texture, glossy and full of life. Long all over the body, including the shoulders. The ruff immense and continuing in a deep frill between the front legs. Ear and toe tufts long. Brush very full.

DISQUALIFY: Locket or button. Kinked or abnormal tail. Incorrect number of toes. Any apparent weakness in the hind quarters. Any apparent deformity of the spine. Deformity of the skull resulting in an asymmetrical face and/or head.*

Persian Colors

The would-be owner of a Persian kitten may find it bewildering to be faced with 39 Persian colors from which to choose. All are decorative, have great charm and usually very good temperaments; they are polite, and answer when spoken to; all make delightful pets.

WHITE: Pure glistening white. <u>Nose Leather and Paw Pads</u>: Pink. <u>Eye Color</u>: Deep blue or brilliant copper. Odd-eyed whites shall have one blue and one copper eye with equal color depth.

There is a slight element of risk in that the Blue-eyed Persian may be deaf, along with the Odd-eyed on the Blue-eyed side. Any white kitten should be carefully checked for deafness before buying. The kittens are pinkish when first born, but in a very short time the fur will grow into a beautiful white coat. They develop rapidly into delightful creatures, much in demand.

Grooming a White is not all that difficult, with talcum powder sprinkled well

* The above listed Disqualifications apply to all Persian cats. Additional disqualifications are listed under Colors.

into the fur and combed and brushed out. The corners of the eyes should be wiped so that there is no staining of the face to spoil the looks. Tails can be a problem as there may be some yellow staining, but it is possible to wash the tail with baby shampoo. Many exhibitors of Whites bathe them a few days before the show, so they have really sparkling coats on the day.

BLACK: Dense coal black, sound from roots to tip of fur. Free from any tinge of rust on tips or smoke undercoat. <u>Nose Leather</u>: Black. <u>Paw Pads</u>: Black or Brown. <u>Eye Color</u>: Brilliant Copper.

Orange-eyed White Persian. This is Shirar Snowman, owned and bred by Mr. and Mrs. G. Martin.

27

These cats look glorious when adult and the lustrous raven-black coats are full and shining. At first sight a Black kitten may disappoint a would-be buyer because frequently the coat may be rusty brown with some white or gray hairs in the fur. As the kitten grows his appearance will change dramatically and he will become a cat of which to be proud. If a Black is to be shown, he must be kept out of strong sunlight and dampness, as these tend to give the fur a brownish tinge. Grooming is the same as for the other longhairs, but a beautiful sheen may be given to the coat by polishing with a soft silk scarf.

BLUE: Blue, lighter shade preferred, one level tone from nose to tip of tail. Sound to the roots. A sound darker shade is more acceptable than an unsound lighter shade. Nose Leather and Paw Pads: Blue. Eye Color: Brilliant Copper.

As this color has been outstanding for many years, the Blues have been used to improve and produce other colors, such as Orange-eyed Whites, Blacks, Creams, and the Himalayans. They are also used in the breeding of Blue-creams. Mated to a Cream female, a Blue male may sire Blue-creams and Cream males: A Blue female mated to a Cream male may have Blue-creams and Blue males, whereas a Blue male mated to a Blue-cream may result in Blue females, Blue-creams, Blue males, and Cream males. The newly born kittens have shadow tabby markings, which rapidly disappear as the fur grows. They are very lively and intelligent. Blues seem to remain kitten-like all their lives; even when as old as 15 years, they will rush around, chasing balls or small toys.

RED: Deep, rich, clear, brilliant red; without shading, markings, or ticking. Lips and chin the same color as coat. Nose Leather and Paw Pads: Brick Red. Eye Color: Brilliant Copper.

This is a rare color, but very striking with rich red flowing fur, with good type. They may be produced from Red Tabbies and are difficult to produce without tabby markings, which are considered a fault. It is often said that all Reds are males. This is untrue, as pure breeding on both sides can produce males and females in the litter. Reds are useful in breeding the female-only color, such as Torties, and have been used in the breeding program for Cameos. Because Persian kittens frequently have tabby markings when first born, it may be difficult for some months to know if a kitten is a true Red Self.

CREAM: One level shade of buff cream, without markings. Sound to the roots. Lighter shades preferred. Nose Leather and Paw Pads: Pink. Eye Color: Brilliant Copper.

A popular color with a full cream fur. By mating Blues and Creams together it is possible to produce Blues, Creams, and Blue-creams in the litters. They are useful too as mates for Blacks and Torties. The type is usually very good. Faults are "hot" coloring on the back and any tabby markings. The numbers are steadily increasing.

CHINCHILLA: Undercoat pure white. Coat on back, flanks, head, and tail sufficiently tipped with black to give the characteristic sparkling silver appearance. Legs may be slightly shaded with tipping. Chin and ear tufts, stomach and chest, pure white. Rims of eyes, lips, and nose outlined with black. Nose Leather: Brick Red. Paw Pads: Black. Eye Color: Green or Blue-Green. Disqualify for incorrect eye color, incorrect eye color being copper, yellow, gold, amber, or any color other than green or blue-green.

Thought to have originated from lightly marked Silver Tabbies, this color is often referred to as the most glamorous of the Persians. Chinchillas are frequently used

Sarasamsan Ragtime Girl, an Odd-eyed White Persian—the different eye colors are clearly visible.

in advertising and their popularity and the numbers bred have greatly increased over the years. When first born, the kittens are very dark, and frequently are a great disappointment to a novice breeder, but as the coat grows it gradually lightens, and often the darkest kitten becomes a prize-winning adult. The type is as for other Persians, but sometimes the heads are not so broad nor the noses so short.

SHADED SILVER: Undercoat white with a mantle of black tipping shading down from sides, face, and tail from dark on the ridge to white on the chin, chest, stomach, and under the tail. Legs to be the same tone as the face. The general effect to be much darker than a chinchilla. Rims of eyes, lips, and nose outlined with black. Nose Leather: Brick Red. Paw Pads: Black. Eye Color: Green or Blue-Green. Disqualify for incorrect eye color, incorrect eye color being copper, yellow, gold, amber, or any color other than green or blue-green.

The distinguishing feature is that the coat is more heavily tipped than that of the Chinchillas, although they may be born in the same litter. The heavy tipping should take the form of a mantle.

CHINCHILLA GOLDEN: Undercoat rich warm cream. Coat on back, flanks, head, and tail sufficiently tipped with seal brown to give golden appearance. Legs may be slightly shaded with tipping. Chin and ear tufts, stomach, and chest, cream. Rims of eyes, lips, and nose outlined with seal brown. Nose Leather: Deep Rose. Paw Pads: Seal Brown. Eye Color: Green or Blue-Green. Disqualify for incorrect eye color, incorrect eye color being copper, yellow, gold, amber, or any color other than green or blue-green.

SMOKE TORTOISESHELL: White undercoat deeply tipped with black with clearly defined, unbrindled patches of red and cream tipped hairs as in the pattern of the Tortoiseshell. Cat in repose appears Tortoiseshell. In motion the white undercoat is clearly apparent. Face and

ears Tortoiseshell pattern with narrow band of white at the base of the hairs next to the skin, which may be seen only when fur is parted. White ruff and ear tufts. Blaze of red or cream tipping on face is desirable. Eye Color: Brilliant Copper.

BLUE-CREAM SMOKE: White undercoat deeply tipped with blue, with clearly defined patches of cream as in the pattern of the Blue-Cream. Cat in repose appears Blue-Cream. In motion the white undercoat is clearly apparent. Face and ears Blue-Cream pattern with narrow band of white at the base of the hair next to the skin that may be seen only when fur is parted. White ruff and ear tufts. Blaze of cream tipping on face is desirable. Eye Color: Brilliant Copper.

CLASSIC TABBY PATTERN: Markings dense, clearly defined, and broad. Legs evenly barred with bracelets coming up to meet the body markings. Tail evenly ringed. Several unbroken necklaces on neck and upper chest, the more the better. Frown marks on forehead form intricate letter M. Unbroken line runs back from outer corner of eye. Swirls on cheeks. Vertical lines over back of head extend to shoulder markings which are in the shape of a butterfly with both upper and lower wings distinctly outlined and marked with dots inside outline. Back markings consist of a vertical line down the spine from butterfly to tail with a vertical stripe paralleling it on each side, the three stripes well separated by stripes of the ground color. Large solid blotch on each side to be encircled by one or more unbroken rings. Side markings should be the same on both sides. Double vertical row of buttons on chest and stomach.

MACKEREL TABBY PATTERN: Markings dense, clearly defined, and all narrow pencillings. Legs evenly barred with narrow bracelets coming up to meet the body markings. Tail barred. Necklaces on neck and chest distinct, like so many chains. Head barred with an M on the forehead. Unbroken lines running back from the eyes. Lines running down the head to meet the shoulders. Spine lines run together to form a narrow saddle. Narrow pencillings run around body.

This Brown Tabby, Persian, Kandyroo Dinky Doo, was once a tiny kitten that had to be hand-reared—now he is a successful show cat. Owner and breeder Mrs. Benge.

PATCHED TABBY PATTERN: A Patched Tabby (Torbie) is an established silver, brown, or blue tabby with patches of red and/or cream.

BROWN PATCHED TABBY: Ground color brilliant coppery brown with classic or mackerel tabby markings of dense black with patches of red and/or cream clearly defined on both body and extremities; a blaze of red and/or cream on the face is desirable. Lips and chin the same shade as the rings around the eyes. Eye Color: Brilliant Copper.

BLUE PATCHED TABBY: Ground color, including lips and chin, pale bluish ivory with classic or mackerel tabby markings of very deep blue affording a good contrast with ground color. Patches of cream clearly defined on both body and extremities; a blaze of cream on the face is desirable. Warm fawn overtones or patina over the whole. Eye Color: Brilliant Copper.

SILVER PATCHED TABBY: Ground color, including lips and chin, pale silver with classic or mackerel tabby markings of dense black with patches of red and/or cream clearly defined on both body and extremities. A blaze of red and/or cream on the face is desirable. Eye Color: Brilliant Copper or Hazel.

SILVER TABBY: Ground color, including lips and chin, pale, clear silver. Markings dense black. Nose Leather: Brick Red. Paw Pads: Black. Eye Color: Green or Hazel.

RED TABBY: Ground color red. Markings deep, rich red. Lips and chin red. Nose Leather and Paw Pads: Brick Red. Eye Color: Brilliant Copper.

BROWN TABBY: Ground color brilliant coppery brown. Markings dense black. Lips and chin the same shade as the rings around the eyes. Back of leg black from paw to heel. Nose Leather: Brick Red. Paw Pads: Black or Brown. Eye Color: Brilliant Copper.

BLUE TABBY: Ground color, including lips and chin, pale bluish ivory. Markings a very deep blue affording a good contrast with ground color. Warm fawn overtones or patina over the whole. Nose Leather: Old Rose. Paw Pads: Rose. Eye Color: Brilliant Copper.

Opposite Grand
Champion Chinchilla,
Adelisa Romulus,
with a good broad
head and magnificent
eye color. Owner
Mrs. Linda Taylor.

CREAM TABBY: Ground color, including lips and chin, very pale cream. Markings of buff or cream sufficiently darker than the ground color to afford good contrast but remaining within the dilute color range. Nose Leather and Paw Pads: Pink. Eye Color: Brilliant Copper.

CAMEO TABBY: Ground color off-white. Markings red. Nose Leather and Paw Pads: Rose. Eye Color: Brilliant Copper.

The colors Brown, Red, and Silver are very popular. All have the same markings—that is, swirls on the cheeks, butterfly markings on the shoulders, pencil marks on the face, deep bands running down the side, and rings on the front of the legs and around the tail. In the three colors the markings are exceedingly difficult to see in the long fur, but, for showing, careful grooming can make the pattern show up.

The Brown Tabby kittens are well marked from birth and are so attractive they are often bought as pets. The Red kittens are glowing little balls of fluff when young and have tabby markings at birth. Sometimes these go and they become Selfs. The Silvers' pattern is more easy to see, but here again it may be some weeks before the true markings are apparent.

SHADED GOLDEN: Undercoat rich warm cream with a mantle of seal brown tipping shading down from sides, face, and tail from dark on the ridge to cream on the chin, chest, stomach, and under the tail. Legs to be the same tone as the face. The general effect to be much darker than a chinchilla. Rims of eyes, lips, and nose outlined with seal brown. Nose Leather: Deep Rose. Paw Pads: Seal Brown. Eye Color: Green or Blue-Green. Disqualify for incorrect eye color, incorrect eye color being copper, yellow, gold, amber, or any color other than green or blue-green.

SHELL CAMEO (Red Chinchilla): Undercoat white, the coat on the back, flanks, head, and tail to be sufficiently tipped with red to give the characteristic sparkling appearance. Face and legs may be very slightly shaded with tipping. Chin, ear tufts, stomach, and chest white. Nose Leather and Paw Pads: Rose. Eye Color: Brilliant Copper.

SHADED CAMEO (Red Shaded): Undercoat white with a mantle of red tipping shading down the sides, face, and tail from dark on the ridge to white on the chin, chest, stomach, and under the tail. Legs to be the same tone as face. The general effect to be much redder than the Shell Cameo. Nose Leather, Rims of Eyes, and Paw Pads: Rose. Eye Color: Brilliant Copper.

SHELL TORTOISESHELL: Undercoat white. Coat on the back, flanks, head, and tail to be delicately tipped in black with well-defined patches of red and cream tipped hairs as in the pattern of the Tortoiseshell. Face and legs may be slightly shaded with tipping. Chin, ear tufts, stomach, and chest white to very slightly tipped. Blaze of red or cream tipping on face is desirable. Eye Color: Brilliant Copper.

SHADED TORTOISESHELL: Undercoat white. Mantle of black tipping and clearly defined patches of red and cream tipped hairs as in the pattern of the Tortoiseshell. Shading down the sides, face, and tail from dark on the ridge to slightly tipped or white on the chin, chest, stomach, legs, and under the tail. The general effect is to be much darker than the Shell Tortoiseshell. Blaze of red or cream tipping on the face is desirable. Eye Color: Brilliant Copper.

BLACK SMOKE: White undercoat, deeply tipped with black. Cat in repose appears black. In motion the white undercoat is clearly apparent. Points and mask black with narrow band of white at base of hairs next to skin which may be seen only when fur is parted. Light silver frill and ear tufts. Nose Leather and Paw Pads: Black. Eye Color: Brilliant Copper.

BLUE SMOKE: White undercoat, deeply tipped with blue. Cat in repose appears blue. In motion the white undercoat is clearly apparent. Points and mask blue with narrow band of white at base of hairs next to skin which may be seen only when fur is parted. White frill and ear tufts. Nose Leather and Paw Pads: Blue. Eye Color: Brilliant Copper.

CAMEO SMOKE (Red Smoke): White undercoat, deeply tipped with red. Cat in repose appears red. In motion the white undercoat is clearly apparent. Points and mask red with narrow band of white at base of hairs next to skin which may be seen only when fur is parted. White frill and ear tufts. Nose Leather, Rims of Eyes, and Paw Pads: Rose. Eye Color: Brilliant Copper.

Very striking colors, with perfect specimens attracting much admiration, the Smokes are comparatively rare and most unusual. They are known as the "cats of contrast" because it is not until they walk that a glimmer of white shows through the dark top coats. At first it is exceedingly difficult for a novice breeder to know if the kittens are Smokes as they look self-colored and it may be many weeks before the contrasts may be seen. These are really striking cats. Grooming is very important so that the undercoat is brushed up to show through the top coat.

TORTOISESHELL: Black with unbrindled patches of red and cream. Patches clearly defined and well broken on both body and extremities. Blaze of red or cream on face is desirable. Eye Color: Brilliant Copper.

CALICO: White with unbrindled patches of black and red. White predominant on underparts. Eye Color: Brilliant Copper.

DILUTE CALICO: White with unbrindled patches of blue and cream. White predominant on underparts. Eye Color: Brilliant Copper.

BLUE-CREAM: Blue with patches of solid cream. Patches clearly defined and well broken on both body and extremities. Eye Color: Brilliant Copper.

This is a female-only variety, with any males proving sterile. Produced from cross-matings with Blues and Creams, and sometimes appearing in Tortie litters, the coat is unusual in that the two pastel colors should be softly intermingled. When first bred in Britain, the coats were very patched and they were often referred to as Blue Torties. In the United States, the standard specifies that the coats be patched, not intermingled. The cross-breeding produces kittens with good type, sturdy and healthy, and much liked for breeding.

BI-COLOR: Black and white, blue and white, red and white, or cream and white. White feet, legs, undersides, chest, and muzzle. Inverted V blaze on face desirable. White under tail and white collar allowable. Eye Color: Brilliant Copper.

PERSIAN VAN BI-COLOR: Black and white, red and white, blue and white, or cream and white. White cat with color confined to the extremities; head, tail, and legs. One or two small colored patches on body allowable.

In the early days of the Cat Fancy, cats with two-colored coats were shown, but these were usually shorthairs. A few longhairs did appear but were invariably neutered as pets. As mentioned earlier, it was then found that Bi-Colors, if correctly bred, could be used to breed the Torties and Whites. At first the standard given was too exacting and few did well at the shows. This was amended and their popularity grew, and they have been Best Cat, Best Longhair, and Best Grand Champion.

PEKE-FACE RED and PEKE-FACE RED TABBY: The Peke-Face cat should conform in color, markings, and general type to the standards set forth for the red and red tabby Persian cat. The head should resemble as much as possible that of the Pekinese dog from which it gets its name. Nose should be very short and depressed, or idented between the eyes. There should be a decidedly wrinkled muzzle. Eyes round, large, and full, set wide apart, prominent and brilliant.

PERSIAN VAN CALICO: White cat with unbrindled patches of black and red confined to the extremities; head, tail, and legs. One or two small colored patches on body allowable.

Shaded Silver, with the silver markings forming a mantle.

PERSIAN VAN DILUTE CALICO: White cat with unbrindled patches of blue and cream confined to the extremities—head, tail, and legs. One or two small colored patches on body allowable. (Note: Cats having more than two small body spots should be shown in the regular Bi-Color Class.)

Himalayan

This exciting breed is a cross-breed from the Blue Persian and the Siamese. The long Persian hair is a recessive trait, as is the Siamese colorpoint.

The Himalayans have light-colored bodies and contrasting points coloring with good longhair type.

Point Score

Head (Including size and shape of 30
   eyes, ear shape and set)
Type (Including shape, size, bone, and . . . 20
   length of tail)
Coat 10
Body Color 10
Point Color 10
Eye Color 10
Balance 5
Refinement 5

HEAD: Round and massive, with great breadth of skull. Round face with round underlying bone structure. Well set on a short, thick neck.

NOSE: Short, snub, and broad. With "break."

CHEEKS: Full.

JAWS: Broad and powerful.

CHIN: Full and well-developed.

EARS: Small, round-tipped, tilted forward, and not unduly open at the base. Set far apart and low on the head fitting into (without distorting) the rounded contour of the head.

EYES: Large, round, and full. Set far apart and brilliant, giving a sweet expression to the face.

BODY: Of cobby type—low on the legs, deep in the chest, equally massive across the shoulders and rump, with a short well-rounded middle piece. Large or medium in size. Quality the determining consideration rather than size.

BACK: Level.

LEGS: Short, thick, and strong. Forelegs straight.

PAWS: Large, round, and firm. Toes carried close, five in front and four behind.

TAIL: Short, but in proportion to body length. Carried without a curve and at an angle lower than the back.

COAT: Long and thick, standing off from the body. Of fine texture, glossy and full of life. Long all over the body, including the shoulders. The ruff immense and continuing in a deep frill between the front legs. Ear and toe tufts long. Brush very full.

COLOR: Body: Even, free of barring, with subtle shading when allowed. Allowance to be made for darker coloring on older cats. Shading should be subtle with definite contrast between points. Points: Mask, ears, legs, feet, tail dense and clearly defined. All of the same shade, and free of barring except for Lynx-Points. Mask covers entire face including whisker pads and is connected to ears by tracings. Mask should not extend over top of head. No ticking or white hairs in points.

PENALIZE: Lack of pigment in nose leather and/or paw pads in part or in total. Any resemblance to Peke-Face.

DISQUALIFY: Locket or button. Any tail abnormality. Crossed eyes. Incorrect number of toes. White toes. Eyes other than blue. Apparent weakness in hind quarters. Deformity of skull and/or mouth.

Himalayan Colors

SEAL POINT: Body even pale fawn to cream, warm in tone, shading gradually into lighter color on the stomach and chest. Points deep seal brown. Nose Leather and Paw Pads: Same color as points. Eye Color: Deep vivid blue.

CHOCOLATE POINT: Body ivory with no shading. Points milk-chocolate color, warm in tone. Nose Leather and Paw Pads: Cinnamon-Pink. Eye Color: Deep vivid blue.

BLUE POINT: Body bluish white, cold in tone, shading gradually to white on stomach and chest. Points blue. Nose Leather and Paw Pads: Slate-colored. Eye Color: Deep vivid blue.

LILAC POINT: Body glacial white with no shading. Points frosty grey with pinkish tone. Nose Leather and Paw Pads: Lavender-Pink. Eye Color: Deep vivid blue.

FLAME (RED) POINT: Body creamy white. Points deep orange flame to deep red. Nose Leather and Paw Pads: Flesh or Coral Pink. Eye Color: Deep vivid blue.

CREAM POINT: Body creamy white with no shading. Points buff cream with no apricot. Nose Leather and Paw Pads: Flesh Pink or Salmon Coral. Eye Color: Deep vivid blue.

TORTIE POINT: Body creamy white or pale fawn. Points seal with unbridled patches of red and cream. Blaze of red or cream on face is desirable. Nose Leather and Paw Pads: Seal brown with flesh and/or coral pink mottling to conform with colors of points. Eye Color: Deep vivid blue.

BLUE-CREAM POINT: Body bluish white or creamy white, shading gradually to white on the stomach and chest. Points blue with patches of cream. Nose Leather and Paw Pads: Slate blue, pink, or a combination of slate blue and pink. Eye Color: Deep vivid blue.

SEAL LYNX-POINT: Points beige-brown ticked with darker brown tabby markings. Body color pale cream to fawn, warm in tone. Mask must be clearly lined with dark stripes vertical on forehead with classic M on forehead, horizontal on cheeks and dark spots on whisker pads clearly outlined in dark color edges. Inner ear light with thumbprint on outer ear. Markings dense, clearly defined and broad. Legs evenly barred with bracelets. Tail barred. No striping or mottling on body, but consideration to be given to shading in older cats. Nose Leather: Seal or Brick Red. Paw Pads: Seal. Eye Color: Deep vivid blue.

BLUE LYNX-POINT: Points light, silvery blue, ticked with darker blue tabby markings. Body color bluish white, cold in tone. Mask must be clearly lined with dark stripes vertical on forehead with classic M on forehead, horizontal on cheeks and dark spots on whisker pads clearly outlined in dark color edges. Inner ear light with thumbprint on outer ear. Markings dense, clearly defined and broad. Legs evenly barred with bracelets. Tail barred. No striping or mottling on body, but consideration to be given to shading in older cats. Nose Leather: Blue or Brick Red. Paw Pads: Blue. Eye Color: Deep vivid blue.

CHOCOLATE SOLID COLOR: Rich, warm chocolate-brown, sound from roots to tip of fur. Nose Leather and Paw Pads: Brown. Eye Color: Brilliant Copper.

LILAC SOLID COLOR: Rich, warm lavender with a pinkish tone, sound and even throughout. Nose Leather and Paw Pads: Pink. Eye Color: Brilliant Copper.

Allowable outcross breeds-Persian.

Note the good blue eyes in this study of a Sealpoint Himalayan, Nickel Estee. Owner and breeder Mrs. L. Saunders.

Taloola d'Artagnan, a Bi-color with good division of the two colors. Owner and breeder Mrs. J. Saunders.

Birman (Sacred Cat of Burma)

These longhair cats should not be confused with the shorthair Burmese. Birmans are said to have originated in the temples of Burma and were introduced into France in the 1920s, where they are known as the Sacred Cats of Burma. The official standard differs from other longhairs as the heads are strong, broad, and rounded; the forehead slopes back and is slightly convex. The ears are medium in length, the nose Roman in shape, with nostrils set low. The coat is long, silken in texture, with heavy ruff around the neck, slightly curly on the stomach. This fur is of such a texture that it does not mat. They have the Siamese coat pattern, that is, light bodies with contrasting points, but with the most distinguishing feature of white paws. The front points are like little white gloves; on the back paws, pure white gauntlets cover the entire paws and taper up the backs to points. They have become very popular both as pets and at the shows.

Point Score

Head (Including size and shape of eyes, ear shape and set)	30
Type (Including shape, size, bone, and length of tail)	25
Coat	10
Color	25
Eye Color	10

HEAD: Skull strong, broad, and rounded. Forehead slopes back and is slightly convex. There is a slight flat spot just in front of the ears.

NOSE: Roman in shape, nostrils set low. Length in proportion to size of head.

CHEEKS: Full. The fur is short in appearance about the face, but to the extreme outer area of the cheek the fur is longer.

JAWS: Heavy.

CHIN: Full and well-developed. Lower lip is strong, forming perpendicular lines with upper lip.

EARS: Medium in length. Almost as wide at the base as tall. Modified to a rounded point at the tip; set as much to the side as into the top of the head.

EYES: Almost round.

BODY: Long but stocky.

LEGS: Medium in length and heavy.

PAWS: Large, round, and firm. Five toes in front, four behind.

TAIL: Medium in length, in pleasing proportion to the body.

COAT: Long, silken in texture, with heavy ruff around the neck, slightly curly on stomach. This fur is of such a texture that it does not mat.

COLOR: Body: Even, with subtle shading when allowed. Strong contrast between body color and points. Points Except Paws: Mask, ears, legs, and tail dense and clearly defined, all of the same shade. Mask covers entire face including whisker pads and is connected to ears by tracings. No ticking or white hair in points. Front Paws: Front paws have white gloves ending in an even line across the paw at the third joint. Back Paws: White glove covers the entire paw and must end in a point, called the laces, that goes up the back of the hock.

PAW PADS: Pink preferred, but dark spot on toe/pad acceptable because of the two colors in pattern.

EYES: Blue in color. The deeper blue the better. Almost round in shape.

PENALIZE: White that does not run across the front paws in an even line. Siamese type head. White shading on stomach and chest.

DISQUALIFY: Lack of white gloves on any paw. Kinked or abnormal tail. Crossed eyes. Incorrect number of toes. Areas of pure white in the points, except paws.

Birman Colors

SEAL POINT: Body even pale fawn to cream, warm in tone, shading gradually to lighter color on the stomach and chest. Points, except for gloves, deep seal brown. Gloves pure white. Nose Leather: Same color as the points. Paw Pads: Pink. Eye Color: Blue, the deeper and more violet the better.

BLUE POINT: Body bluish white, cold in tone, shading gradually to almost white on stomach and chest. Points, except for gloves, deep blue. Gloves pure white. Nose Leather: Slate-color. Paw Pads: Pink. Eye Color: Blue, the deeper and more violet the better.

Gr Ch Mister Jubilee:
a Blue Himalayan.
Owner Miss Monika
Forster; breeder Mrs.
Pat Rawlins.

Opposite Grand
Premier Sealpoint
Birman, Strathdean
Saroki Chio. Owner
and breeder Mrs. T.
Cole.

CHOCOLATE POINT: Body ivory with no shading. Points, except for gloves, milk-chocolate color, warm in tone. Gloves pure white. Nose Leather: Cinnamon-Pink. Paw Pads: Pink. Eye Color: Blue, the deeper and more violet the better.

LILAC POINT: Body a cold, glacial tone verging on white with no shading. Points, except for gloves, frosty grey with pinkish tone. Gloves pure white. Nose leather: Lavender-Pink. Paw

Pads: Pink. Eye Color: Blue, the deeper and more violet the better.

Turkish Angora

In the sixties, Colonel and Mrs. W. Grant brought two pairs of Turkish Angoras to America. The breed is solid and firm, giving the impression of grace and flowing movement. There are now a number of coat colorings, although the White still seems to be the favorite.

Point Score

Head 35
Body 30
Color 20
Coat 15

GENERAL: Solid, firm, giving the impression of grace and flowing movement.

HEAD: Size, small to medium. Wedge-shaped. Wide at top. Definite taper toward chin. Allowance to be made for jowls in stud cat.

EARS: Wide at base, long, pointed, and tufted. Set high on the head and erect.

EYES: Large, almond shaped. Slanting upwards slightly.

NOSE: Medium long, gentle slope. No break.

NECK: Slim and graceful, medium length.

CHIN: Gently rounded. Tip to form a perpendicular line with the nose.

JAW: Tapered.

BODY: Small to medium size in female, slightly larger in male. Torso long, graceful, and lithe. Chest, light framed. Rump slightly higher than front. Bone, fine.

LEGS: Long. Hind legs longer than front.

PAWS: Small and round, dainty. Tufts between toes.

TAIL: Long and tapering, wide at base, narrow at end, full. Carried lower than body but not trailing. When moving relaxed tail is carried horizontally over the body, sometimes almost touching the head.

COAT: Body coat medium-long, long at ruff. Full brush on tail. Silky with a wavy tendency. Wavier on stomach. Very fine and having a silk-like sheen.

BALANCE: Proportionate in all physical aspects with graceful lithe appearance.

DISQUALIFY: Persian body type. Kinked or abnormal tail.

Turkish Angora Colors

WHITE: Pure white, no other coloring. <u>Paw Pads and Nose Leather</u>: Pink. <u>Eye Color</u>: Odd-Eyed, Blue-Eyed, Amber-Eyed.

BLACK: Dense coal black, sound from roots to tip of fur. Free from any tinge of rust on tips or smoke undercoat. <u>Nose Leather</u>: Black. <u>Paw Pads</u>: Black or Brown. <u>Eye Color</u>: Amber.

BLUE: Blue, lighter shade preferred. One level tone from nose to tip of tail. Sound to the roots. A sound darker shade is more acceptable than an unsound lighter shade. <u>Nose Leather and Paw Pads</u>: Blue. <u>Eye Color</u>: Amber.

CREAM: One level shade of buff cream without markings. Sound to the roots. Lighter shades preferred. <u>Nose Leather and Paw Pads</u>: Pink. <u>Eye Color</u>: Amber.

RED: Deep, rich, clear, brilliant red; without shading, markings, or ticking. Lips and chin the same color as coat. <u>Nose Leather and Paw Pads</u>: Brick Red. <u>Eye Color</u>: Amber.

BLACK SMOKE: White undercoat, deeply tipped with black. Cat in repose appears black. In motion the white undercoat is clearly apparent. Points and mask black with narrow band of white at base of hairs next to skin which may be seen only when fur is parted. <u>Nose Leather and Paw Pads</u>: Black. <u>Eye Color</u>: Amber.

BLUE SMOKE: White undercoat, deeply tipped with blue. Cat in repose appears blue. In motion the white undercoat is clearly apparent. Points and mask blue with narrow band of white at base of hairs next to skin which may be seen only when fur is parted. <u>Nose Leather and Paw Pads</u>: Blue. <u>Eye Color</u>: Amber.

CLASSIC TABBY PATTERN: Markings dense, clearly defined, and broad. Legs evenly barred with bracelets coming up to meet the body markings. Tail evenly ringed. Several unbroken necklaces on neck and upper chest, the more the better. Frown marks on forehead form intricate letter M. Unbroken line runs back from outer corner of eye. Swirls on cheeks. Vertical lines over back of head extend to shoulder markings which are in the shape of a butterfly with both upper and lower wings distinctly outlined and marked with dots inside outline. Back markings consist of a vertical line down the spine from butterfly to tail with a vertical stripe paralleling it on each side, the three stripes well separated by stripes of the ground color. Large solid blotch on each side to be encircled by one or more unbroken rings. Side markings should be the same on both sides. Double vertical row of buttons on chest and stomach.

MACKEREL TABBY PATTERN: Markings dense, clearly defined, and all narrow pencillings. Legs evenly barred with narrow bracelets coming up to meet the body markings. Tail barred. Necklaces on neck and chest distinct, like so many chains. Head barred with an M on the forehead. Unbroken lines running back from the eyes. Lines running down the head to meet the shoulders. Spine lines run together to form a narrow saddle. Narrow pencillings run around body.

SILVER TABBY: Ground color, including lips and chin, pale clear silver. Markings dense black. <u>Nose Leather</u>: Brick Red. <u>Paw Pads</u>: Black. <u>Eye Color</u>: Green or Hazel.

RED TABBY: Ground color red. Markings deep rich red. Lips and chin red. <u>Nose Leather and Paw Pads</u>: Brick Red. <u>Eye Color</u>: Amber.

BROWN TABBY: Ground color brilliant coppery brown. Markings dense black. Lips and chin the same shade as the rings around the eyes. Back of leg black from paw to heel. <u>Nose Leather</u>: Brick Red. <u>Paw Pads</u>: Black or Brown. <u>Eye Color</u>: Amber.

Maine Coon

These cats originated in Maine more than 100 years ago and were thought to have resulted from longhair cats, brought in by sailors and merchants, intermating with the resident shorthairs. Massive, strong, and healthy, the Maine Coons have longish fur, but not so luxuriant as that of the Persians. At first mostly Brown Tabbies with some white, their popularity has rap-

With their distinctive auburn markings, a Turkish mother and her kitten: Erevan Kayisi, and Erevan Benim. Owner and breeder Mrs. Sims.

idly spread and now all colors and coat patterns are permitted. The name "Coon" was given as it was once thought they were bred by cats and raccoons mating, but this is not possible.

Point Score

HEAD (30)
    Shape 15
    Ears 10
    Eyes 5
BODY (35)
    Shape 20
    Neck 5
    Legs and Feet 5
    Tail 5

COAT (20)
COLOR (15)
    Body Color 10
    Eye Color 5

GENERAL: Originally a working cat, the Maine Coon is solid, rugged, and can endure a harsh climate. A distinctive characteristic is its smooth, shaggy coat. With an essentially amiable disposition, it has adapted to varied environments.

HEAD SHAPE: Medium in width and medium long in length with a squareness to the muzzle. Allowance should be made for broadening in older studs. Cheek bones high. Chin firm and in line with nose and upper lip. Nose medium long in length; slight concavity when viewed in profile.

45

Cream Shaded Cameo, Snowzetta Polperro, with white undercoat and cream tips. Owner and breeder Mrs. N. Boyle.

EARS: Large, well-tufted, wide at base, tapering to appear pointed. Set high and well apart.

EYES: Large, wide set. Slightly oblique setting.

NECK: Medium long.

BODY SHAPE: Muscular, broad-chested. Size medium to large. Females may be smaller than males. The body should be long with all parts in proportion to create a rectangular appearance. Allowance should be made for slow maturation.

LEGS AND FEET: Legs substantial, wide set, of medium length, and in proportion to the body. Paws large, round, well-tufted. Five toes in front; four in back.

TAIL: Long, wide at base, and tapering. Fur long and flowing.

COAT: Heavy and shaggy; shorter on the shoulders and longer on the stomach and britches. Frontal ruff desirable. Texture silky with coat falling smoothly.

PENALIZE: A coat that is short or overall even.

DISQUALIFY: Delicate bone structure. Undershot chin. Crossed eyes. Kinked tail. Incorrect number of toes. Buttons, lockets, or spots.

Maine Coon Colors

EYE COLOR: Eye color should be shades of green, gold, or copper, though white cats may also be either blue or odd-eyed. There is no relationship between eye color and coat color.

Solid Color Class

WHITE: Pure glistening white. Nose Leather and Paw Pads: Pink.

BLACK: Dense coal black, sound from roots to tip of fur. Free from any tinge of rust on tips or smoke undercoat. Nose Leather: Black. Paw Pads: Black or Brown.

BLUE: One level tone from nose to tip of tail. Sound to the roots. Nose Leather and Paws Pads: Blue.

RED: Deep, rich, clear, brilliant red; without shading, markings, or ticking. Lips and chin the

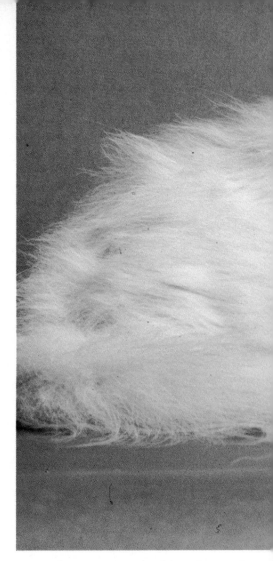

same color as coat. Nose Leather and Paw Pads: Brick Red.

CREAM: One level shade of buff cream, without markings. Sound to the roots. Nose Leather and Paw Pads: Pink.

Tabby Color Class

CLASSIC TABBY PATTERN: Markings dense, clearly defined and broad. Legs evenly barred

with bracelets coming up to meet the body markings. Tail evenly ringed. Several unbroken necklaces on neck and upper chest, the more the better. Frown marks on forehead form an intricate letter M. Unbroken line runs back from outer corner of eye. Swirls on cheeks. Vertical lines over back of head extend to shoulder markings which are in the shape of a butterfly with both upper and lower wings distinctly out-lined and marked with dots inside outline. Back markings consist of a vertical line down the spine from butterfly to tail with a vertical stripe par-alleling it on each side, the three stripes well separated by stripes of the ground color. Large solid blotch on each side to be encircled by one or more unbroken rings. Side markings should be the same on both sides. Double ver-tical row of buttons on chest and stomach.

MACKEREL TABBY PATTERN: Markings dense, clearly defined and all narrow pencillings. Legs evenly barred with narrow bracelets coming up to meet the body markings. Tail barred. Necklaces on neck and chest distinct, like so many chains. Head barred with an M on the forehead. Unbroken lines running back from the eyes. Lines running down the head to meet the shoulders. Spine lines run together to form a narrow saddle. Narrow pencillings run around the body.

SILVER TABBY: Ground color pale, clear silver. Markings dense black. White trim around lip and chin allowed. Nose Leather: Brick Red desirable. Paw Pads: Black desirable.

RED TABBY: Ground color red. Markings deep, rich red. White trim around lip and chin allowed. Nose Leather and Paw Pads: Brick Red desirable.

BROWN TABBY: Ground color brilliant coppery brown. Markings dense black. Back of leg black from paw to heel. White trim around lip and chin allowed. Nose Leather and Paw Pads: Black or Brown desirable.

BLUE TABBY: Ground color pale bluish ivory. Markings a very deep blue affording a good contrast with ground color. Warm fawn overtones or patina over the whole. White trim around lip and chin allowed. Nose Leather: Old Rose desirable. Paw Pads: Rose desirable.

CREAM TABBY: Ground color very pale cream. Markings of buff or cream sufficiently darker than the ground color to afford good contrast but remaining within the dilute range. White trim around lip and chin allowed. Nose Leather and Paw Pads: Pink desirable.

CAMEO TABBY: Ground color off-white. Markings red. White trim around lip and chin allowed. Nose Leather and Paw Pads: Rose desirable.

PATCHED TABBY PATTERN: A Patched Tabby (Torbie) is an established silver, brown, or blue tabby with patches of red and/or cream.

Tabby With White Class

TABBY WITH WHITE: Color as defined for Tabby with or without white on the face. Must have white on bib, belly, and all four paws. White on one-third of body is desirable. Colors accepted are Silver, Red, Brown, Blue, or Cream.

PATCHED TABBY WITH WHITE (Torbie with White): Color as described for Patched Tabby (Torbie) but with distribution of white markings as described in Tabby with White. Color as described for Patched Tabby (Torbie) with or without white on face. Must have white on bib, belly, and all four paws. White on one-third of body desirable. Colors accepted are Silver, Brown, or Blue.

Parti-Color Class

TORTOISESHELL: Black with unbrindled patches of red and cream. Patches clearly defined and well broken on both body and extremities. Blaze of red or cream on face is desirable.

TORTOISESHELL WITH WHITE: Color as defined for Tortoiseshell with or withhout white on the face. Must have white on bib, belly, and all four paws. White on one-third of body is desirable.

CALICO: White with unbrindled patches of black and red. White predominant on underparts.

DILUTE CALICO: White with unbrindled patches of blue and cream. White predominant on underparts.

BLUE-CREAM: Blue with patches of solid cream. Patches clearly defined and well broken on both body and extremities.

BLUE-CREAM WITH WHITE: Color as defined for Blue-Cream with or without white on the face. Must have white on bib, belly, and all four paws. White on one-third of the body is desirable.

BI-COLOR: A combination of a solid color with white. The colored areas predominate with the white portions being located on the face, chest, belly, legs, and feet. Colors accepted are Red, Black, Blue, or Cream.

Other Maine Coon Colors Class

CHINCHILLA: Undercoat pure white. Coat on back, flanks, head, and tail sufficiently tipped with black to give the characteristic sparkling silver appearance. Legs may be slightly shaded with tipping. Chin, ear tufts, stomach, and chest, pure white. Rims of eyes, lips, and nose outlined with Black. Nose Leather: Brick Red. Paw Pads: Black.

SHADED SILVER: Undercoat white with a mantle of black tipping shading down from sides, face, and tail from dark on the ridge to white on the chin, chest, stomach, and under the tail. Legs to be the same tone as the face. The general effect to be much darker than a Chinchilla. Rims of eyes, lips, and nose outlined with black. Nose Leather: Brick Red. Paw Pads: Black.

SHELL CAMEO (Red Chinchilla): Undercoat white, the coat on the back, flanks, head, and tail to be sufficiently tipped with red to give the characteristic sparkling appearance. Face and legs may be very slightly shaded with tipping. Chin, ear tufts, stomach, and chest white. Nose Leather, Rims of Eyes, and Paw Pads: Rose.

SHADED CAMEO (Red Shaded): Undercoat white with a mantle of red tipping shading down the sides, face, and tail from dark on the ridge to white on the chin, chest, stomach, and under the tail. Legs to be the same tone as face. The general effect to be much redder than the Shell Cameo. Nose Leather, Rims of Eyes, and Paw Pads: Rose.

BLACK SMOKE: White undercoat, deeply tipped with black. Cat in repose appears black. In motion the white undercoat is clearly apparent. Points and mask black with narrow band of white at base of hairs next to skin which may be seen only when fur is parted. Light silver frill and ear tufts. Nose Leather and Paw Pads: Black.

BLUE SMOKE: White undercoat, deeply tipped with blue. Cat in repose appears blue. In motion the white undercoat is clearly apparent. Points and mask blue with narrow band of white hairs next to skin which may be seen only when fur is parted. White frill and ear tufts. Nose Leather and Paw Pads: Blue.

CAMEO SMOKE (Red Smoke): White undercoat, deeply tipped with red. Cat in repose appears red. In motion the white undercoat is clearly apparent. Points and mask red with narrow band of white at base of hairs next to skin which may be seen only when fur is parted. Nose Leather, Rims of Eyes, and Paw Pads: Rose.

Turkish

Similar in type to the original Angoras, to which they must have been related, these cats were introduced into Britain some years ago direct from the Van area of Turkey. Compared with most other longhair varieties, the heads are wedge-shaped rather than round, the ears large, and the noses long. The bodies, too, are longish and the tails medium length. The eyes are light amber color. Turkish cats differ from the original Angoras in that although the long silky fur is also chalk-white, they have auburn markings on the face and auburn tails with faint rings. In hot weather they seem to shed their coats, sometimes appearing almost shorthaired. In Turkey they are known to swim in warm pools and shallow rivers.

The kittens, even when newly born, have distinct auburn markings. They develop early, are highly intelligent, and make decorative pets, devoted to their owners.

From Britain they have been sent all over the world; the numbers at American shows are not increasing greatly.

Cameos

These beautiful cats were first bred in the United States in 1954 from Smoke and Tortoiseshell matings. There are five color variations: Shell, Shaded, Red Smoke, Tortie Cream, and Blue Cream. The undercoats are white, with tippings and shadings of red and cream. The Red variations are as follows: the Shell is lightly

The correct shadings are just appearing in this Shaded Silver Persian kitten, Chirunga Silver Mist. Owner and breeder Mrs. Kayes.

tipped with rose pink; the Shaded, with red shading, gives the effect of a red mantle; the Smoke has red shading on the sides and face, and a red mask and feet; the Tortie has black, red, and cream tipping, broken into patches. In the Cream, there is Shell, the Shaded, and the Smoke, with Cream replacing the Red, and also a Blue-cream Cameo with blue and cream intermingled tipping. The eyes in all variations should be orange or copper. The type is for other longhairs, with broad head, small ears, and so on. The cross-breeding has produced pretty cats with very good type who are very attractive in appearance.

4 The Longhairs as Pets: Acquisition and Care

You may be thinking of having a longhair kitten as a pet and have seen or read about the many delightful varieties there are available. Before even considering any particular one, it is advisable to consider the advantages and the disadvantages of owning such a pet.

It should be remembered that a twelve-week-old adorable bundle of fluff will rapidly grow into an equally lovable but very large cat that will need daily grooming to keep that immaculate look, and which will certainly live a long life, maybe as long as 20 years given care, affection, and good mixed feeding. He will have to be fed two or three times a day, and if there is no garden, will need the litter tray changed constantly. When holiday time comes around arrangements will have to be made for his welfare. The development of his character will depend very much on the attention and the time you give to him when young. In return for this you will have a charming pet that will give you constant companionship and affection and be a most decorative addition to your home.

Because of their short noses and flat faces, which tend to give the longhairs an aloof and aristocratic look, they are sometimes thought to be bad-tempered. This is not true; generally they have quieter temperaments and are less noisy than some of the shorthair varieties. If you are away from home all day it is really better not to have a young kitten, but you could consider taking on an older cat needing a home from one of the animal shelters. A happy solution is to buy two kittens which will be companions for one another and try to come home at midday to feed them, or to get a neighbor to come in to see that everything is all right.

If you buy two kittens to grow up together, and they are different sexes, they should be neutered at the age recommended by the vet, otherwise you may become a breeder unwittingly. When you buy a kitten as a pet it does not really matter about the sex, as it is advisable to have it neutered in any case. If a male is allowed freedom, when old enough he will travel for miles seeking likely females and may return with torn ears and bleeding wounds, having been involved in fights with other males. He will undoubtedly make the house smell with his strong tomcat odors, even spraying indoors. A female will come into season as soon as she is developed enough and will need to be constantly watched to see that she does not get out and get mated with the local Romeo. Some female longhairs are far from noisy when in season but a few

Some things are better done in private.

may really howl and even upset the neighbors, as well as attract any roving male that may be around.

The best age for neutering will largely depend on the kitten's development, and the vet will advise on this. Generally a male cat can be altered or castrated (testicles removed) when the testicles are visible, that is, after about six months. It is not a complicated procedure, when done under total anaesthesia by a qualified veterinarian. Anaesthetics are also given for spaying a female cat, as it is a more serious operation involving major surgery. Spaying can best be done shortly after the cat has had her first estrus cycle (after her first heat), which is usually between the fifth and sixth month. The operation (ovariohysterectomy) will be a little more serious, as she will have two or three stitches, and will need a few days' nursing.

Obviously a garden is best for a cat to use as a toilet, but cats can live happily in an apartment, using litter boxes and with pots of grass to chew, to prevent fur balls. An enclosed balcony would make an ideal sun-bathing spot.

Once having decided which variety of longhair kitten you would like, it is not always easy to find one. The best plan is to visit a cat show, see the different kinds, talk to the breeders, and maybe order a kitten. It is not advisable to buy one straight from a show, as even if the kitten is inoculated against feline infectious enteritis (and it must have been to be allowed in the show), there are still other illnesses that can be picked up and that may not be apparent for a few days. There are several useful periodicals that carry advertisements for kittens: *Animals Magazine*, MSPCA, 350 South Huntington Avenue, Boston, MA 02130; *Cat Fancy Magazine*, P.O. Box 2431, Boulder, CO 80321; *Cats Magazine*, P.O. Box 83048, Lincoln, NE 68501; and others. A new monthly magazine, *The Cat Fanciers' Almanac*, is also available from the CFA.

If possible visit the breeder's house and see the way the animals are kept. If given the choice of a litter, choose a lively and energetic kitten, with big bright eyes, clean ears, and fur that stands away from the body, whose little tail is held upright, with no signs of diarrhea underneath. The kitten should be sturdy and well fed, with well-groomed fur and no signs of flea dirts. He should be at least twelve weeks old and housetrained.

Collect the kitten in a suitable container, as it is inadvisable to have a young kitten on the lap when taking it in a car. Some kittens take it all quite calmly but others may panic, missing the mother and usual surroundings. Some may dribble and others may mew all the time, but in closed containers with warm blankets, they may not notice the unaccustomed motion of the car so much; they may even settle down and sleep until arriving in the new home.

At home have a cosy bed ready. You may buy one of those especially made for kittens but a small cardboad box with newspaper and a blanket is ideal to start. This could be under a cupboard or a table in a corner where the kitten will feel secure and can hide if scared. Place the litter pan on newspaper near the bed at first, using the litter recommended by the breeder. Peat can be used but this does get scattered around, and unless changed constantly earth does get very muddy.

Put the kitten in one room at first, making sure that all the windows and doors are closed and the chimney blocked, or closely guarded if there is an open fire. It may never have seen a fire in its short

Blue-cream Persian. This is Lafrebella Julie. Owner Mrs. I. Harding; breeder Mrs. I. Bangs.

life and will not appreciate the danger. Allow the kitten plenty of time to inspect the new home and do not keep picking it up or allowing young children to do so. The young bones are very fragile and are easily broken or injured if the kitten is squeezed or dropped. Grooming should be a daily routine. You will need a soft brush, a wide-toothed comb, and a narrow-pronged one to remove dirt and the possible odd flea.

It will be an easy task at first to groom the small fluffy kitten, but a grown cat with a very full coat will be a different matter, needing at least 20 minutes each day, or even two such sessions during the spring and fall when the coat is being shed and knots up quickly. Some cats do not take kindly to being brushed and combed, especially on the stomach. If this is the case, little and often is the rule. Have ready a little cotton wool to wipe the corners of the eyes and inside the ears to remove any dust that may collect. Comb through the coat with the wide-toothed comb and brush well. The fur around the head should be brushed up to form a frame for the face. This is known as the ruff or frill. With a light coat, a little baby talcum powder sprinkled in the fur and brushed out thoroughly will remove any grease.

Finding a suitable name can be difficult. If the kitten is already registered it will have a pedigree with its name on it. This will bear the breeder's cattery name, for example Bluestar and then a name, which could be Playboy for a male or Honey for a female. If you do not like the given name, you can always give the kitten a pet name to which he will answer readily in a day or two. If the kitten is not already registered, the breeder may be able to use the name you suggest along with the cattery prefix.

The kitten will require four small meals a day, which should follow the diet sheet given you by the breeder. This should be maintained for the first few weeks with any new item introduced a little at a time and the effect noted. A change of home may cause a slight digestive upset resulting in diarrhea or constipation. In the case of diarrhea, cut down on the liquids and sprinkle on the food a little kaolin, easily obtained from a pharmacist. In the case of constipation, serve food with a teaspoonful of vegetable oil. The diet may include scraped raw beef, cooked meat such as lamb, rabbit, chicken, a little liver or heart, with a few cornflakes or brown bread mixed with it for roughage. Boned, cooked white fish may be included but not all cats are fish lovers. It is important to give a mixed diet and too much fish can cause eczema. There are excellent canned foods on the market, which are very good when the kitten is older, and there are also those made particularly for kittens. Not all kittens can take cow's milk as it may cause looseness, but others drink it with no ill effects; however, evaporated milk is better. Porridge, rice pudding, or one of the prepared baby foods are also good. A few vegetables may also be given. Bones of any kind should not be included, as they may splinter and cause internal damage.

Kittens' stomachs are very small, and about a tablespoonful each of the four meals should be sufficient, with the amounts being increased as the kitten grows. At about six months the meals may be cut down to three, and at about a year old, to two. It is advisable to give as varied a diet as possible, as not only will it provide all that is necessary for the kitten to grow up strong and healthy, but it will also ensure that it will not be too fussy if

a certain item cannot be obtained. There should always be clean water on the floor for drinking. This is essential, for milk is a food not a drink. The kitten should always have access to grass for chewing which acts as an emetic and helps to prevent fur ball. A weekly dose of a teaspoonful of liquid paraffin or vegetable oil will also be helpful for this, as well as daily grooming to remove any loose hairs. If there are other pets, say another cat or a dog, introduce them slowly, and never leave them alone together for the first week or so; thereafter they should begin to accept one another. Feed the pets separately and make an extra fuss of the resident animals, so that they are not jealous. Give plenty of toys, such as toy mice and small balls, so that the kitten gets plenty of exercise. After the grooming session try to play with the kitten, giving it special attention. This will make it look forward to being groomed.

If your kitten was not inoculated against feline infectious enteritis before you bought it, this should be done as soon as it has settled down and before it comes into contact with other cats. FIE, as it is known, is a killer illness. Once it is contracted there is little hope of recovery, but inoculation does give almost 100 percent immunity. The symptoms are varied, with low temperature, vomiting, deterioration in general condition, lassitude, and perhaps diarrhea. It is vital that the vet be called in at once, as death can follow in a few hours. If this does happen, another kitten should not be brought into the house for at least six months. Cat flu (also known as feline viral rhinotracheitis, or FVR) is a disease which affects the nasal passages. It is very contagious and can be picked up at any time and early veterinary treatment is essential. At first it may be

suspected that the cat has just caught cold, as there may be a high temperature and running nose and eyes, with coughing and sneezing. The cat may become listless and lose its appetite. Good nursing is essential, as is an even temperature. There are several vaccinations available against cat flu, but because there are a number of different viruses, complete immunity can never be guaranteed.

Another worrying illness is Feline leukemia (FeLV). It is a cancerous infectious disease of the lymphatic system, caused by an oncornavirus. In layman's terms, it is a virus that causes cancer of the white blood cells and in the cells of lymph tissue. The virus is mainly transmittable from an infected cat to another cat by saliva. Infection is therefore principally possible through close contact.

A patient lacks all appetite, has a dry coat and loses weight fast. As the virus remains infectious only while *in* the body, it can be easily destroyed by disinfectants when outside the cat's body for a period of time. It is essential to seek early medical treatment, especially as an infected cat may develop other forms of leukemia, lymphosarcoma (tumors of the various organs), anemia, and intestinal and kidney disorders. A veterinarian will do blood smears and X-rays, among other medical procedures, in order to establish a diagnosis. It is important to know that the discovery of a preventive vaccination may be realized in the very near future. But until we have this vaccination, it is advisable to visit the veterinarian regularly to ensure that your cats are free of this dangerous disease.

The Feline urologic syndrome (FUS) is, as the name implies, a group of interconnected illnesses. FUS starts with *cystitis,* an inflammation of the interior of the

The Somali (this is Harvey Wallbanger) resembles an Abyssinian with a longer coat—it is one of the "foreign" varieties. Owner Miss Jacqui Murphy; breeders the Somali Breeders' Society.

Dogs and cats become excellent companions if brought up together. This Balthazar Chinchilla Persian kitten is owned and bred by Mrs. C. Philbrick.

bladder, caused by bacteria. The patient runs a fever and urinates frequently, with pain and great difficulty. The cat usually cries and may vomit, definitely in the latter stage. The urine is clouded by pus (red blood cells, albumin, and other organic material). It now becomes possible for the urine to remain in the bladder and become concentrated (*urolothiasis*). The inflammation of the bladder becomes more serious, and tiny stones and sandy particles (*struvite*) are mixed with the clouded urine, forming larger "plugs." These plugs accumulate in the urethral passage so that the urine flow becomes very slow or even stops altogether (*urethral obstruction*). Because the patient is unable or barely able to urinate, the kidneys stop functioning properly and poisonous wastes remain in the body (*uremia*). When the obstructions are not relieved—through veterinarian treatment—lethal poisoning is the result. Many speculations as to what causes FUS are known; among others are dry cat food, vitamin deficiency, low water intake, and a narrow urethra in tomcats. It is advisable to see your veterinarian as soon as it becomes apparent that your cat has difficulties urinating properly. The majority of the patients respond satisfactorily to the treatment, and only in chronic cases may surgery be necessary.

It is always important to ensure that your cat is flea free, as fleas can be responsible for worms, skin diseases, and anemia. Any animal can pick up the occasional flea, but daily grooming and the use of a good flea collar should keep these pests at bay. These collars contain a slow-release insecticide. Some cats may be allergic to the chemicals, and it is therefore advisable to wait 24 hours after releasing the chemicals (often by pulling on both ends of the collar) before use. Kittens up to ten weeks

59

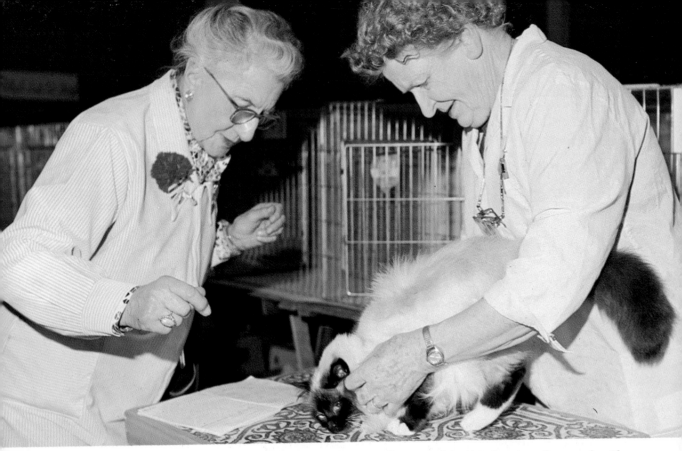

In Britain the judges and stewards go to the cat's cage to carry out the judging.

of age are not allowed to wear a collar; in any case read the instructions on the package carefully, and when in doubt about what to use or how to fight fleas and ticks, ask your veterinarian.

Cats who live in the country may pick up ticks, which are rather horrible. Greyish-blue in appearance, they hang on to the cat's skin by the head, sucking the blood until bloated to the size of a pea. Flea powders are useless, and each tick must be first of all dabbed with surgical spirit, and then removed without pulling, as removal may otherwise leave the head embedded in the cat's body, causing a sore. The cat's skin should be dabbed with a mild disinfectant afterwards. If not removed, ticks can cause anemia.

Lice are sometimes found on cats. These are pale grey and flat. They attach themselves to the cat, laying their eggs, referred to as nits, in the coat, causing the cat to keep scratching. Treatment is the same as for fleas, but may need to be repeated weekly until all trace of them is gone. They can be picked off with tweezers.

Tapeworms can be caused by fleas or if a cat kills and eats rats and mice. Segmented and flat, they may look like flat, dry grains of rice in the fur under the tail and as segments in the movements. The head attaches itself to the intestine, and the body can grow up to several feet in length. Tapeworms cause rapid loss of condition, irritation, and swollen stomachs. Modern treatment ordered by the vet will easily clear up the condition, but it should be repeated in a few weeks to ensure that the tapeworm has gone completely.

Roundworms may be seen in the movements, looking like thin spaghetti, and varying from one-half inch to three inches in length. They affect kittens and cats, kittens in particular, causing the fur to look spiky and the tummy swollen, and the haws may be up in the corners of the eyes. It is important that you get correct medicine from your vet, as indiscriminate worming has been the death of many a young kitten. The vet will probably recommend piperazine which has been used safely for many years. A second dose should be given after two weeks to ensure that no larvae have been left.

If a cat or kitten keeps shaking its head and scratching its ears, examine the ears carefully. There may be a nasty smell and a slight discharge which is caused by ear mites. Very tiny, they are not easy to see without a magnifying glass. Usually referred to by the layman as canker, they need specific treatment by a vet. If the condition is very bad, he may wash the ear out and recommend ear drops to be given daily. If there are other animals in the household, their ears should be looked at as well, since the mites can easily be passed from one animal to another.

There are several skin diseases which cats may get. These include eczema, which is not contagious, and can take various forms. It may be caused by an allergy, for example, to excessive fish or even milk. Ringworm is very contagious, and can be passed on to humans by a cat or vice versa.

It can be picked up from infected rats or mice. Bald roundish patches may be seen in the fur. The animal should be isolated and handled with rubber gloves, and an overall worn when treatment is administered. The cat's bedding and anything he sleeps on should be replaced. Modern treatment, which can only be prescribed by a vet, should be started as soon as possible.

Longhair cats will sometimes vomit a small sausage-shaped wad of fur, which is referred to as furball or hairball. This may happen after chewing grass, which is a natural emetic and should always be available. Daily grooming to remove the old hairs, which otherwise the cat would swallow when washing, and a weekly dose of corn or similar oil or liquid paraffin should prevent the accumulation of fur inside; it could otherwise form a solid mass which would cause problems.

Rabies is a terrifying disease, invariably fatal, and known in many parts of the world. It affects most mammals, but primarily dogs and wildlife (bats, foxes, raccoons, and skunks). Because rabies is a public health problem, state health departments have done a great deal to help control or eliminate this dreaded viral disease, which affects the central nervous system of the animal. In Britain and Hawaii, where rabies does not exist, there are rigid and strict quarantine laws. It is also important to know that in order to cross over some state lines, a health certificate provided by an approved veterinarian is required. Therefore, it is essential to check on local regulations.

The majority of longhair cats and kittens are extremely healthy, living long happy lives, and rarely needing a vet's services, but it should be remembered that booster inoculations are given for feline infectious enteritis.

5 Breeding

If considering breeding, as a beginner you should spend plenty of time visiting shows, speaking to the exhibitors, walking around the hall, and looking at the kittens. You should buy a catalog and make a note of the prizewinners and others in the same class and see if you agree with the judges' choices. This may well help you make up your mind as to which variety you would like to breed. Try to make an appointment to go to a breeder's house and see the animals there. If you do see a kitten that you like when visiting the house, be quite honest about the fact that you intend to breed from any kitten that you are likely to buy. It is unfair to imply that you are just looking for a pet, although your kitten will probably also be treated as your pet. The price for a pet kitten and one with good future breeding potential can vary considerably. It is better to buy a kitten as near to the recognized standard as possible, and the best you can afford. Ask the breeder to tell you the good and bad points of a kitten, particularly if you intend to show. If possible ask to see the mother, and the male if he is there as well, so you will have an idea of what the adult cat will be like. Ask to see the pedigree. Even if full of Champions, it will probably mean little to you, but a good pedigree does show that the kitten has been bred from good stock, and may well eventually produce a future Champion,

even if she never becomes a Champion herself.

You must look on breeding as a pleasant hobby for it will certainly not be a paying one, with the cost of feeding, stud fees, injections, and possibly other veterinary bills. If you do get bitten with the breeding bug you will find that three or four well-kept and loved females living as house pets will do better than large numbers kept in an outdoor cattery.

The age at which your female will start calling is very difficult to predict. Some come into season when only five months old, and others at seven or eight months, or as late as a year. An average age for the longhairs is about six months, but at that age she will not be developed enough to be mated. Ten months is old enough for mating, and only then if it is her second call, at least. It may be difficult to know when she is calling, as not all longhairs are noisy, but some of them certainly let everybody know. The first sign is usually excessive friendliness, with the cat following her owner around, probably letting out little plaintive mews, rubbing against her owner's legs, then rolling on the ground and eventually padding up and down on the floor with the back legs. She may start really yelling, so much so that the alarmed owner may think that she is in terrible pain. A close examination under the tail will show that the vulva

A Cream Persian stud with excellent type— this is Barwell Timothy. Owner Mrs. Pullen.

is swollen and there is a slight discharge. This may not be noticed if a cat is always washing herself. The length of the call may vary considerably from cat to cat and can be from about two or three days up to about ten. The time between the calls varies too, some cats calling every month, some every two or three months, and others only once a year. A careful watch will have to be kept on the queen, as she may use every endeavor to get out, and hopeful males may be waiting outside making determined efforts to get in!

Choosing the stud, for which an appointment should be made well in advance, is very important. Not only should he be a very good example of the variety, correcting any faults which the female may have, and looking well fed and well groomed, but the conditions under which he is kept should also be seen, if possible. Ask to see the actual house your cat will be put in to get to know the male. The stud fee will have to be paid in advance when the female goes there. If by any chance the mating does not take, and no kittens result, a second mating may be given later, but this is not obligatory. The cat must have had a feline infectious enteritis certificate and some stud owners also insist on a certificate certifying that she is free of feline infectious leukemia. The stud fee will vary according to the male's status. For a Champion it may well

This Silver Tabby Persian shows the correct coat markings. Ch. Santiago Silver Sosa. Owner Mrs. V. Chard; breeder Mrs. J. Massie.

be high and for a Grand Champion higher still.

It is advisable to check with local officials when a cat must travel by public transportation (train, bus, airline) as regulations differ from area to area. Be aware of the fact that cats travelling by plane must do so in specially designed carriers prescribed by the individual airline.

Your cat will be at the stud owner for at least three days or longer, and then you will have to arrange for her return. Once home again she must be well guarded and kept indoors until the calling has stopped, which may be a week or more. If allowed out beforehand she may meet another male and a dual mating could happen, with kittens by both the stud and the rogue male being born in the same litter. This is a pity but would in no way affect her future breeding. Before going to stud, she should have been wormed out, and naturally she should be flea free. Do not treat her as an invalid on her return; allow her to exercise and give a good mixed diet. At about the sixth week give an extra midday milk feed. After three weeks the first signs of a succesful mating may be seen with the nipples turning pink. About the fifth or sixth week, a definite swelling of the sides may be noticed. The period for gestation is about 65 days, but may vary by a day or two. A few weeks before the kittens are due prepare a kittening box, which could be of tough cardboard, with the bottom covered with plenty of newspaper, which she may well shred up, almost making a nest. It is better to put in a thick blanket after the kittens are born. To make things easier for the female, near the date of the birth clip the fur away from around the nipples, being careful not to nip her, to make suckling easier, and from around the vulva to make

the births cleaner. As kittening time grows nearer she will have to be watched to ensure that she does have the kittens in the box provided and not in your bed or in a drawer full of clean linen. She may well be restless, wanting her owner around, and there may be signs of milk in the nipples. The first sign that the kittens are imminent may be a kind of bubble protruding from her rear. Most cats manage everything on their own, washing the kit-

tens and cleaning up, but should she seem to be in distress, straining for some time with nothing happening, it is advisable to telephone the vet. In any case, for a first litter it is well to notify your vet of the approximate date in case his help is required, although this rarely happens.

The kittens are born one at a time in separate transparent sacs which should be broken by the mother by tearing with her teeth, releasing the kitten which she will start washing immediately. If she does not tear the sac, this can be done quite easily and gently by tearing around the head with a fingernail. The kittens are born attached by the umbilical cord to the placenta or afterbirth. The mother bites through the cord and usually eats the placenta. There should be one for each kitten. If she does not eat it and the cord is still attached, cut with sterilized scissors about 1½ inches from the navel, and dis-

Tortoiseshell and White Persians are another female-only variety: here is Sarasamsan Foxfire, with striking, bright coloring. Owner and breeder Mrs. S. Corris.

more kittens, remove the newspapers, which may be dampened and stained, and without disturbing the mother too much, put her in the blanket, with all the kittens under her. Give her a warm drink and a light meal if she will take it, and leave the little family to settle down quietly.

Longhairs are not so prolific breeders as some shorthairs, with four kittens being about the average, but six or seven can occur. Two litters a year is enough and many breeders allow only one.

If you wish to know the sex of the kittens, this may be established a day or two after the birth, before the fur grows too much, if the mother has no objection to having her kittens handled. Handle the kittens with care as they are only about the size of mice. In the female will be seen a small slit, which is the entrance to the vagina, close to the anus under the tail, while the male has a circular anus near the base of the tail, with rudimentary testicles about half an inch away. If the male and female are held close together the difference may be clearly seen. If the mother appears to have plenty of milk, with the kittens suckling contentedly and sleeping most of the time, they will need little attention for the first week or two. If one seems undersized after a day or two, it should be examined carefully to see that everything is normal, and if it is, the rest of the litter can be taken away while the small one has an extra feed, or supplementary feeding may be given in a tiny feeding bottle, using evaporated milk or a baby food. The eyes should open when about twelve days old, but should there be a slight discharge, smear the lids with a little Vaseline. Should they look swollen and fail to open, consult your vet. The mother cat should be given extra meals and milky drinks while feeding her family.

pose of the placenta. The kitten should start breathing and giving a little mew as she washes it. Sometimes the kittens arrive very quickly and it is advisable to have a wrapped hot water bottle in a small box standing by to put the first ones on while she is coping with the next birth. Be careful not to put the kittens on to a too-hot, unprotected bottle. The kittens are born blind but in a matter of minutes make their way to the nipples by instinct and start suckling, padding away with their paws, which helps to stimulate the flow of milk. When it appears that there are no

When three weeks old weaning may start with a few drops of baby food in a small spoon. One kitten may well refuse to show any interest while another will try to lick it up right away. Gradually baby cereal may be added, and a few drops of milk of magnesia to aid digestion, and two meals given a day. At five weeks, scraped raw beef, minced chicken or rabbit, boned and mashed cooked white fish, and baby foods may be given. Do not over-do it, for the mother will still be feeding them as well. Never rush the weaning, as the supply of mother's milk should be allowed to reduce gradually; otherwise she may get an abscess through a blockage. She should be willing to leave the kittens for a while and her milky feeds should be stopped and water given to drink (which should have been there for her all the time). By the age of eight to nine weeks the kittens should be completely

Lamplighters Leola, a blue-and-white Bi-color, owned and bred by Mrs. O'Donohughe.

67

weaned and used to a variety of foods, having four to five small meals a day.

When the kittens are about three weeks old, put down a small litter tray. After being shown it once or twice kittens seem to toilet train themselves, but the tray must be kept clean and changed frequently.

They should be ready to be sold when about twelve weeks old, but a week or two before this it may be advisable to advertise them in cat magazines or local newspapers. If you are interested in showing and wish to become known as a breeder, you may care to exhibit one of the best when at least thirteen weeks old. Wins at shows may well bring in orders for any future kittens.

Comparatively few fanciers put a male at public stud these days, although there are a few. A stud will have to be really outstanding if you intend to use him for visiting queens as well as your own females. It should be remembered too that it will almost certainly be necessary to provide a house and large run for him in the garden, well away from neighbors who will complain about the noises that may come from there. Before taking on a stud, it is well to go to a local library and read as much as possible about keeping a male and the housing it will need. It is not an easy way to make money. Hours will be spent in a stud house as all matings should be supervised to ensure that they have taken place. Some queens can be very difficult, although some are very easy. The first mating for a young stud cat should be with an experienced queen.

The points coloring is just appearing in these Himalayan kittens, from Mrs. P. Pye's Venn cattery.

6 Cat Clubs and the Cat Fancy

The clubs are the lifeline of the Cat Fancy. If there were no clubs there could not be a pedigree Cat Fancy. There are eight national Cat Registry Organizations, of which the Cat Fanciers' Association (CFA) is the largest, with many affiliated clubs. Besides authorizing cat shows across the United States, CFA controls a nationwide scoring system for the cat winnings in its affiliated clubs' shows. CFA also trains and appoints judges. And if this is not enough, CFA produces each year a handy, well-written and organized (almost encyclopedic) *CFA Yearbook*.

The governing cat bodies are:
American Cat Association, Inc.
Susie Page
10065 Foothill Boulevard
Lake View Terrace, CA 91342

American Cat Fanciers' Association, Inc.
Edward Rugenstein
P.O. Box 203
Point Lookout, MO 65726

Cat Fanciers' Association, Inc.
Walter A. Friend, Jr., President
1309 Allaire Avenue
Ocean, NJ 07712

Cat Fanciers' Federation, Inc.
Ms. Barbara Haley
9509 Montgomery Road
Cincinnati, OH 45242

Crown Cat Fancier's Federation
Mrs. Martha Underwood
1379 Tyler Park Drive
Louisville, KY 40204

International Cat Association (TICA)
Bob Mullen
211 East Olive, Suite 201
Burbank, CA 91502

United Cat Federation, Inc.
David Young
6621 Thornwood Street
San Diego, CA 9211

It is important to know that there are reciprocal arrangements between the United States' governing bodies for cats and the Canadian Cat Association (CCA), which means that qualified American cats can enter and compete in the Canadian shows, and, of course, vice versa. The address of the CCA is:

Canadian Cat Association
Donna Aragona
14 Nelson Street W., Suite 5
Brampton, Ontario
Canada L6X 1B7

Self Chocolate Persians are another recent variety—here is Etoile Chocolate Fancy, with a good coat. Owner and breeder Miss S. L. Booth.

One of the newest varieties, the Self Lilac Persian with its delicate coloring. The photograph shows Trefleur Lilac Limerick. Owner Miss S. L. Booth; breeder Miss E. Eade.

Below Red Shaded Cameo; shown here is Holdenhurst Pink Floyd. Owner and breeder Mrs. S. Butler.

Any show gives a novice as well as an experienced fancier an excellent opportunity to learn all about showing and, of course, cats! Novice cat enthusiasts see how an animal behaves when being handled. There may be also opportunities to talk to breeders and judges, and to ask them about the cats in the show. The majority of the shows attract a large entry, and a novice must look at them as excellent training, as they of course are, both for the exhibitor and the exhibit.

If you intend to go in for breeding and showing, it is a good idea to join a club and get to know members with similar interests. Some clubs run social events to help raise funds, and also arrange talks and teach-ins. Meetings are held where

members are elected to the committees and other offices. Joining a club is the first step in becoming involved in the Cat Fancy, by helping at shows, at the awards tables, and so on, and ultimately becoming a judge, although this may take some years.

A breed club will look after the interest of a particular variety, hold Championship shows, and generally care for anything relating to this color or breed. As planned breeding programs bring new colors into being, invariably new clubs will form to promote them and draw up standards that perhaps will eventually be passed by the appropriate body.

The clubs will encourage members to become involved in breeding programs; indeed the clubs are the lifelines of the Cat Fancy. If there were no clubs, there could be no pedigree Cat Fancy!

Red Himalayan with a good mask and points—Ch. Nickel Topas, owned and bred by Mrs. L. Saunders.

Index
Page numbers in *italics* refer to illustrations